The Transcendent Ape
An evolutionary journey through religion, mysticism, cults, and other human foibles

Pyotr Patrushev

"The Transcendent Ape" by Pyotr Patrushev © 2018

All rights reserved. No part of this publication may be reproduced, distributed, or transmitted in any form or by any means, including photocopying, recording, or other electronic or mechanical methods, without the prior written permission of the publisher, except in the case of brief quotations embodied in critical reviews and certain other non-commercial uses permitted by copyright law.

Illustrations by Slava Fiantsev © 2017-2018

Front cover image, sculpture by Hugo Rheinhold
[© 2006 Axel Schmetzke]

First Edition

ISBN:
978-0-6926806-3-6

Published by

Leaf Garden Press, 2018
LeafGardenPress.com

in association with

Peganum Books, 2018
www.pyotr-patrushev.com

To my son Andrei:

Turn the page, tune in, and dwell
in your stardust-seeded body.

Do it, now.

Contents

Introduction	1
Prologue	7
Chapter 1. The "Sacred Disease" and Other Paranormal States	17
I. The Varieties of Epileptic Experience: Seizures, Saints, and Sex	17
II. In the Beginning, there was the Rhythm	33
III. But what do I love, when I love Thee?	40
IV. The Inside out of Abnormality	53
Chapter 2. The Sanskrit Cookbook	73
I. To Seize the Moment…	73
II. The Way of the Simple Regard	83
III. To Scour the Windows of the Soul	90
IV. The Yogi and the Wolf	97
V. Non-attachment	99
Chapter 3. Modern Messiahs	107
I. J. Krishnamurti	107
II. Transcendental Meditation (TM)	116
III. Primal Therapy	127
IV. Hare Krishna	148
Epilogue	155
About the extraordinary life of Pyotr Patrushev	163
References	168

Introduction

On the day that Pyotr Patrushev completed this draft of *The Transcendent Ape* he had a stroke and soon died in March 2016, aged 73. For this reason, he was unable to complete its final editing. This however, does not detract from its unique and original perspective.

The Transcendent Ape is the product of a lifetime of reflection on the human condition, and the paradox that our highest ideals are constantly thwarted by our behaviour and failure to live up to what we aspire to. As the title suggests, this book's starting point is the rapid evolution of a peculiar primate, *homo sapiens*. Over the past couple of million years, we have been engaged in an extraordinary co-evolution of mind and culture that has allowed us to dominate life on this planet and also given us the capacity to destroy ourselves and rest of life in the process.

This short book, while not a work of satire, embodies many of the characteristics of Voltaire's 'Candide', in its wry exploration of our pretensions and follies. It is the product of an astute author who spent a good part of his career as a science journalist, working for both the BBC and Radio

Liberty in Europe and US during the ideological insanity of the Cold War when he interviewed the most brilliant minds of his time.

Pyotr, as he explains in his autobiography *Prigovoren k Rastrelu* [Sentenced to death] (Patrushev, 2005), escaped from Russia as a young man by swimming to Turkey through the heavily patrolled Black Sea in the 1960's, and was later sentenced to death in absentia by the Communist regime.

Perhaps, as a consequence of his need to escape from the mental straightjackets imposed on both sides of the Cold War ideological battle front, Pyotr developed a life-long interest in science, and also in the growing understanding of the links between our behaviour, perception and what goes on in our brains. This interest, as it had done for Aldous Huxley[a], led him to research Eastern religious ideas and meditation practices.

Pyotr's first novel *Project Nirvana - How the War on Drugs was Won* (Patrushev, 2014) was a satirical account of a Soviet effort to win the Cold War by developing state-controlled drugs to enhance productivity when used with meditation. This and much more provided a practical recipe for reaching world peace while simultaneously ending the futile war on drugs.

Self-transcendence is the essential theme of this book, which in the first section reviews the various means that individuals and communities have used to gain what the religious describe as spiritual powers. In fact, what Pyotr's research suggests is that many of humanity's earliest

---

[a] See Huxley's *The Doors of Perception*, *The Perennial Philosophy* and *Brave New World* (Huxley, 2006, 2009, 2013).

experiences of transcendence were probably the by-product of epileptic fits or brain seizures of one sort or another produced by the consumption of inappropriate fungi and other natural intoxicants.

Anthropologists working in all parts of the world, including in Pyotr's native Siberia, have reported on the practice of Shamans using alcohol, toxic fungi, and other brain-altering substances, to induce trance states which were believed to provide contact with the realm of the gods, and the capacity to draw on their healing and spiritual powers. It is only now, however, with advances in neuroimaging, such as PET scanning, that we can begin to understand the actual link between brain states produced by epileptic fits, and those induced by hallucinogenic drugs and religious experience. Pyotr provides in the first section of this book convincing evidence that many of our messianic and religious leaders suffered from fits, or were able to induce such conditions. The pursuit of such states of altered consciousness seems to have been an almost universal characteristic of human communities and played a significant role in the emergence of religious beliefs be they animistic, pantheistic or monotheistic.

A critical phase in this part of our cultural evolution was the shift from hunter-gatherers to agriculturalists and with it the discovery of fermentation processes, and particularly the production of alcohol. Equally significant was the accidental exposure to potent hallucinogenic toxins such as ergotamine (and its by-product lysergic acid) produced when the Claviceps purpurea fungus gets into stored and damp rye grain. There have been numerous cases of mass hysteria, beginning with records from the later middle ages, in communities where outbreaks of visions of angels and demons, and possession by spirits occurred, particularly in early spring, around Easter or Lent. At this time, there was little remaining food in many rural communities, and they were forced to make bread from the remains of their damp stores of rye grain. Ergotamine poisoning can occur from eating bread made from this fungus-infected rye.

While such phenomena were not uncommon in settled agrarian communities, the consumption of toxic or hallucinogenic fungi and plants was also common when food supplies were low. These then came to be used in religious rituals, particularly by the aborigines of Siberia, where Pyotr was born and raised. So, whether by accident or design, the use of consciousness-altering substances has played a significant role in the lives, not just of hippies seeking psychedelic experiences in the 1960's, but of people throughout much of human history. The desperate need to have insight into the arbitrary forces of 'chance and necessity' that shape our daily lives, the desire to summon the gods or to be in communion with them has been the foundation of how we have navigated life and death, illness and health. Above all this need has also helped induce the mental states that underpinned the mystical foundations of both religious belief and cultural behaviour. It has also provided an escape from existential anguish, poverty and social injustice.

The Transcendent Ape follows this tradition into its modern incarnations by exploring our continuing attraction to the mind-altering practices, therapies and cults that have abounded throughout the 20th century. From Asian mysticism and meditation practices to therapies such as primal screaming, such practices seem to provide a release from the existential complexity of modernity. In analyzing the drives that have led many to seek new modes of self-transcendence, this book provides a valuable insight not only into the evolution of our minds but also humanity's extraordinary capacity for self-delusion.

The evolutionary foundations of this propensity lie in the complex structure of our neurophysiology, which is only now beginning to be understood. It is an understanding that cannot come too soon, as we stand on the brink of the 'Anthropocene era' of global development, in which we, *homo sapiens*, fundamentally shape life on this planet. However, the dilemma that Pyotr finally leaves us to ponder is whether the nature of this 'life' in the future will be shaped more by our need for self-transcendence, or by our moral and rational capacity to accept responsibility for the quality of the life we create and leave for future generations. It is that ancient classical dilemma of balancing the Apollonian and Dionysian aspects of our personalities, which Pyotr, like Nietzsche, struggled with throughout his life.

John Merson,
University of NSW, 2017

Prologue

I was born in Siberia, on the doorstep of the Gulag, at the beginning of the Second World War. My father was killed early in the war, which I only later recognized as the deranged fight between two not too dissimilar ideologies (Communism and Fascism), led by two fatherless sons (Stalin and Hitler) who both hated authority and covered their sociopathic urges under the lofty pretext of ideology.

My mother was a Russian Orthodox believer, whose faith consisted mostly of superstitions and following some simple church rules. There was an icon of a stern Byzantine Christ in the corner of our main room. I was baptized but was quickly brainwashed at school into becoming an atheist. However, really, the subject of religion did not figure much during my childhood. Survival, mostly at the level of hunting and gathering (mushrooms, berries and nuts) was our main preoccupation, with some trading in produce and pickles to procure much-needed cash.

I read avidly as a boy, loved science, and also literature. I read mostly Russian classics, as well as English and French authors available in translation. I enjoyed humour and satire. My favourite Russian authors were Ilf and Petrov the two Soviet satirists, and my favourite foreign author was Jerome K. Jerome. This love of humour and satire stayed with me for life and is, hopefully, reflected in the book you are about to read.

By the time I was 14, I was ready to leave home to strike out on my own in a big city.

Having gained access to some fine libraries in the university city of Tomsk, I read everything from Freud to the early sociological treatises of Emile Durkheim. They were hopelessly dated of course, but they provided a breath of fresh air compared to the stale diet of Marx and Engels, about the steady progression from tool-making hominid to steadfast and victorious proletarian toiler.

I got into trouble with the authorities over my anti-war views and had to get out of the country in a hurry. Before I fled, I read the Bible, which was hard to procure, the latest religious writings of Leo Tolstoy and the Buddhist scripture of *Dhammapada*. In confronting the persecution and the threat of physical annihilation after my escape by swimming out of Russia, being sentenced to death on charges of "high treason" and being put on the KGB's wanted list for 27 years I pondered the meaning of human life (or lack of such) in concrete and immediate terms. The ancient scriptures, with their perennial wisdom, and Leo Tolstoy's dedication to spiritual life and ideology of non-violence had a profound impact on me.

After my escape, I was fortunate to get a job as a journalist, first for the BBC in London, and later for Radio Liberty in Munich, where I authored my own science shows. I read avidly and interviewed some of the leading scientists of the day. My deepening spiritual quests lead me first to Transcendental Meditation and later to Buddhism. I met and interviewed many gurus and teachers for my shows. Gradually, as I learned to look behind the façade of the official spiritual teachings, I discovered the human face of the various cults, and my scepticism grew. However, I respected the humane and humanitarian aspects of the work of some of the gurus and mystics I have met (notably Krishnamurti, see Chapter 3 for more).

However, it was Arthur Koestler (1982), with his *The Ghost in the Machine* who had led me to evolution and the theories of the "Triune Brain" as expounded by Paul D. MacLean (1971, p. 342). I know that MacLean's theory of the triune brain is now questioned by some neurophysiologists on technical grounds, but the larger picture remains: we have remnants of earlier evolutionary structures in our brain and their genesis is as relevant to the way we function as the development of our skeletons is relevant to the prevalence of hernias and back pain in modern humans.

As I began to delve into the detail of religious experiences and cults, I did it from an evolutionary perspective (Spuhler, 1973, pp. 39-46). Thus, the cults I chose to write about were selected from a multitude of others because they were significant in terms of the peculiar ways in which they attempted to remedy human suffering. Thus, Primal Therapy was based on an extreme form of "abreaction" (emotional release) that penetrated many therapies and cults, from psychoanalysis to snake handling (Shovron & Sargant, 1947, 709-732). The Hare Krishna cult is a sociological phenomenon, with a strong element of "devotion" mixed in, which makes it similar to many charismatic movements and many traditional religions in their extreme manifestations. Jiddu Krishnamurti was really a fundamentalist Zen teacher (and a person with epilepsy) and probably the most compassionate and rational of modern gurus and teachers. His insights, coming from the mind that was "opened up" by epilepsy, were suprarational; they gave him an air of authority and, one could argue, stubbornness bordering on haughtiness. Maharishi Mahesh Yogi was typical of many Indian cult gurus in their attempts at westernization and finding a "scientific" validation for their teachings.

Many books cover evolution in greater and more recent detail, and there are many treatises on individual cults and various forms of religious mysticism. My book is an insider's journey, as well as that of an objective/scientific observer. It is not written by an Oxford don with the view of discrediting points of view that are non-compliant with the latest scientific research; nor is it a passionate rave of a rationalist who abhors the seeming stupidity and cruelty of organized traditional religions. It is, instead, a record of a personal search for the answer to "the predicament of man". For Arthur Koestler who coined this term, it was the conflict between the aggressive and the altruistic tendencies in man, between reason and emotion-based beliefs. This "schizophrenic split" led to our identification with various ideologies that ultimately resulted in truly murderous sprees, from human sacrifice to religious wars and genocide. In *The Ghost in the Machine* (1990), Koestler spoke of a human "delusionary streak running through history."

I describe the human predicament in the bigger framework of evolutionary history: that of a mammal and a primate who was subjected to extraordinary selective pressures that led to his survival in the current form, with the potential for genocide and ecocide, as well as for the highest artistic and intellectual achievement. The unique blend of these qualities and how they manifest themselves in our attempts to remedy "the split" (the origin of the word religion is after all "religere," which is to bind or even to reconnect), is the subject matter of the book.

Our great 60,000,00th grandma,
some 160 million years ago. (Adobe collection).

It was a Greek philosopher Zeno of Citium (333-262 BC) who said that "All things are parts of one single system, which is called Nature."

The ancestral line that led to modern humans was subjected to *extraordinary selection pressures*. During the mammalian explosion after the demise of the dinosaurs, the ancestors of man, the tiny nocturnal mammals, missed the early escape route that birds took from the toothy competition on the ground.

Therefore, we did the next best thing: climbed into the trees. However, when the big drought came, and the primeval forests shrunk, we had to descend to the ground again, where our enemies became even toothier and more fleet-footed. That was truly the time of the proverbial Fall, accompanied by much "wailing and gnashing of the teeth." At a number of points, we came close to extinction. At first, we survived mostly through scavenging and cannibalism. We are the unlikely survivors of an evolutionary detour into the trees that almost ended up as a pile of bones on the dry African savannah. However, the brain and the group-derived flexible communication skills, challenged by these extraordinary pressures, grew exponentially.

Primate. (Fiantsev, 2017)

It must be very flattering for a terrestrial primate to think of himself as being on some glorious cosmic journey. It is so easy to forget that his brain and mind evolved on the African savannah, fuelled by fire, tempered by scavenging and cannibalism, and honed by hunting and warfare.

It can be argued that humans could have self-destructed long ago, had they not contained, within their genome, the bonobo strain that could manifest under certain relatively benign conditions. Bonobos are one of humankind's closest living relatives, sharing more than 99% of our DNA. They differ in morphology, behavior and even emotions and cognition from chimpanzees, our other aggressive ancestor. It may be indicative of our perilous future that both the bonobo gene pool and their meme are today under a severe threat, due to the continuous onslaught on both by hostile forces (i.e. poachers on the one hand, and politicians/arms peddlers practising the unmitigated notion of a competitive "killer ape," on the other).

**We share 98% of our genes
(and many behavioral traits) with bonobos.** (Adobe collection).

**And more aggressive and territorial
common chimpanzees.** (Adobe collection).

It is heartening to see that the _Big History Project (2016)_, a web portal looking at the human journey in the context of large-scale evolution is gaining ground and is available to anyone for online study as well as in many schools and universities.

However, to understand how evolution has shaped us into the planetary force that we are, for good or evil, we have to understand the reasons for our ancestors' escape up into the trees and their arboreal habitat and then their descent back down to earth millions of years later into an inhospitable and dangerous environment.

This book attempts to explain the phenomenon of how two critical bottlenecks in the history of human evolution and the fault lines in our brain and mind have resulted in acute longing for the return to heavenly paradise through religion, spirituality and cults.

Chapter 1.
The "Sacred Disease" and Other Paranormal States

I. The Varieties of Epileptic Experience: Seizures, Saints, and Sex

Epilepsy is Nature's way of conducting neurological experiments. The wide variety of phenomena associated with the epileptic seizure can teach us a great deal about how certain brain functions affect our perception and behaviour.

The history of epilepsy as a recognized condition presents one with a truly confusing picture. On the one hand, it has been nearly always associated in the popular mind with such things as demon possession, sorcery, ability to prophesy and so on. A story from the Bible immortalizes this attitude to the "sacred disease." A man brings his son to Jesus to be healed and says: "Master, I have brought unto thee my son, which hath a dumb spirit: And wheresoever he taketh him, he teareth him: and he foameth, and gnasheth with his teeth and pineth away" (Mark 9:17, 18). Jesus then "rebuked the foul spirit, saying unto him, 'Thou dumb and deaf spirit, I charge thee come out of him, and enter no more into him.' And the spirit cried, and rent him sore and came out of him: and he was as one dead... But Jesus took him by the hand, and lifted him up and he arose."

On the other hand, the first treatise on epilepsy available to us, written 2500 years ago by the Greek physician Hippocrates, refers to epilepsy as the "so-called sacred disease" (Hippocrates, 1923) and attempts to give this condition a purely scientific explanation. Therefore, this curious conflict between the popular and enlightened opinion continues to the present day: physicians have been trying to assure the lay public that epilepsy is caused by "cold fumes rising from the head" (medieval explanation), or "abnormal, excessive electrical discharges of neurons" (modern explanation). The lay public listened politely, but still continued to view the "falling sickness" with fascination, awe, and sometimes fear and hostility (Temkin, 2010, p. 26).

The amount of suffering this attitude inflicts on people afflicted by epilepsy must be staggering. An ancient historian tells us that one way in which the disease used to be diagnosed was to put the suspect into a goat's skin, plunge him into the sea, and observe whether he sank or not. If he did, the diagnosis was confirmed (similar fates were reserved for people accused of witchcraft). Even during more enlightened times (the last third of the 18th century) castration and clitoridectomy were still considered to be of good therapeutic value in cases of stubborn epilepsy since this disease was sometimes thought to be caused by the "pernicious habit" of masturbation. The practice of trephining (making a hole in the skull) was also attempted to correct some cases of epilepsy and may have possibly been practiced for this purpose even in prehistoric times.

However, not all the past attitudes about epilepsy have such gloomy overtones. At certain times epilepsy was associated with special gifts such as high intelligence or creativity. Perhaps the best-known advocate of this view was the Spanish psychiatrist Cesare Lombroso (1835-1909), (Lombroso, 2016). He wrote of numerous men of genius seized by motor epilepsy. Among these were: Moliere, Julius Caesar, Petrarch, Peter the Great, Mahomet, Handel, Swift, Richelieu, Charles V, Flaubert, Dostoyevsky and St. Paul (Lombroso, 1891, p. 337).

Here, of course, Lombroso has stretched the definition of epilepsy a bit too far in some cases or based his diagnoses on hearsay or scanty evidence. Another author who gave epilepsy a very prominent place in society was Tommaso Campanella. In his Utopian *City of the Sun* (Ernst, 2010), quite a number of citizens were epileptics. Campanella describes epilepsy as a sign of great talent, wherefore Hercules, Socrates, Mohammed, Scotus and Callimachus suffered from it.

All this leads us to ask, what is our current understanding of epilepsy? It comprises such a number of diversified conditions that a simple and straightforward answer to the question of its origin seems impossible. In one book on epilepsy, the classification table contains 27 separate types of seizures, the last one being "unclassified." Most commonly, all epilepsies are subdivided into three clearly distinguishable types: "grand mal" (in French – big sickness), "petit mal" (little sickness), and "psychomotor epilepsy."

The *grand mal* seizure is what people most often associate with epilepsy. It is accompanied by convulsions of the whole body and loss of consciousness. Sometimes immediately before the attack, the *grand mal* epileptic emits a shrill cry caused by sudden contraction of the breathing apparatus. The seizure then proceeds automatically through the "tonic" phase, in which the patient turns blue in the face and is immobile, to the final "clonic" phase, in which his limbs start jerking, and he may experience incontinence and tongue-biting. There is nothing much one can do about the fit until it has run its full course, usually in a few minutes.

A *petit mal* fit is also known as a "short absence," which conveys the nature of the disorder. A person who suffers from this type of epilepsy may be engaged in some task when, all of a sudden, his consciousness lapses and he will have a "blank" period generally lasting only a few seconds. During the blank period, many victims also remain conscious, suffering partial numbness to the face or limbs and loss of the ability to communicate. It may happen a dozen, or in some severe cases, several hundred times a day. Children are particularly prone to this type of epilepsy.

The last type of epilepsy is called "psychomotor" (or "temporal lobe," or "limbic"). It is more widespread than the previous two varieties. Perhaps 60% of all epileptic seizures are psychomotor. Like all epileptic fits, they are often preceded by a peculiar sensation, which is called, an "aura" and which is usually repeated before every attack.[b]

---

[b] In Greek, the meaning of "aura" is "breeze." A young patient of a famous Greek physician Galen described a peculiar feeling of an aura ascending from his legs to his head as a "cold breeze."

Vincent Van Gogh was an epileptic. (Adobe collection).

After experiencing the aura, the psychomotor epileptic becomes unresponsive and may indulge in some automatic, compulsive (like moving things randomly on the table) or even aggressive behaviour. There is, however, one more feature associated particularly with psychomotor epilepsy that is of special interest to us. *Sometimes the "aura" experienced by people with epilepsy is associated with very powerful sensations of bliss and tranquillity which are usually interpreted within a religious framework and which often lead to cases of sudden religious conversion.* An 18th-century English scholar described a typical case of an apprentice boy who was badly beaten over the head by his tutor and acquired epilepsy which eventually led to "ecstasies" (Magnus & de Haas, 1974, 295–301):

As soon as he was out of a fit, the first thing he would do was to sing diverse songs and hymns (though it was not known that he had ever learnt any) very melodiously. From this singing, he would now and then pass abruptly to some strange relations, but especially of such and such, lately dead, whom he had seen in Paradise; and then fall to singing again. But when he was perfectly come to himself, and had left singing, then would he sadly and with much confidence maintain that he had been, not upon his bed, as they that were present would make him believe; but in heaven with his Heavenly Father, having been carried thither by Angels and placed in a most pleasant green, where he had enjoyed excessive happiness, and had seen things that he could not express (Temkin, 2010, p. 26).

By the middle of the 19th century, a sufficient number of such accounts were accumulated to convince some historians of the basic similarity between these epilepsy-provoked religious revelations and the supposedly authentic ones (Tart, 1972, pp. 1203-10). A typical case in question is that of Mohammed. When the circumstances of his famous conversion were shown to be indicative of epilepsy, some scholars denounced him as a fraud. The more moderate critics realized, however, that a person with epilepsy is completely convinced of the reality of his vision and should, therefore be at least given credit for honesty.

Another famous case of revelation through an epileptic fit is that of Dostoyevsky (Horváth, 2011, pp. 69-95). He described how his first attack and accompanying revelation occurred. The night before Easter Sunday, Dostoyevsky (who was then in exile) spent the whole night with a close friend arguing hotly about the question of God's existence. The friend was an atheist, Dostoyevsky, a believer, and both were firmly convinced in the veracity of their views. Becoming excited, Dostoyevsky shouted: "God exists, yes he does!" At this very moment, the air around them became filled with the ringing of the bells in a neighboring church.

"And I felt," Dostoyevsky tells, "that the sky had descended on earth and swallowed me. The nature of God was directly revealed to me and became part of me." "Yes, God exists!" he shouted and lost his consciousness (Dostoyevsky in Memoirs of his Contemporaries, 1923).

Dostoyevsky was preoccupied with the religious experiences of Mohammed in which he found parallels to his own. He also clearly indicated that the most important feature of his aura was indescribable bliss. He emphasized that this sensation of bliss had an intensity which would be completely incomprehensible to those who knew only "earthly joys" (Frank, 1987). There is even an air of haughtiness when Dostoyevsky talks about his experiences:

All you, healthy people... you don't even suspect what real happiness is, that happiness which we, epileptics, experience during that second which precedes the fit. Mohammed tries to tell us in his Koran that he really saw paradise and visited it. All the clever fools are convinced that he is just a liar and a fraud. Oh no! He is no liar! He really was in paradise during epilepsy from which he, like myself, suffered. I do not know whether this bliss lasts seconds, hours, or months, but believe my words, I would not forfeit it for all the joys which life can offer (Walter, 1963, p. 92).

This idea of the profound superiority of bliss experienced during epilepsy, compared to that found in ordinary life, was so embedded in Dostoyevsky's mind, that whenever he brought this subject up in his novels, he would reiterate it almost verbatim. In his novel *The Idiot*, the epileptic Prince Myshkin exclaims to himself: "Yes, for this moment, one can give away all of one's life." (Dostoevsky, 2016, p. 214).

In another novel by Dostoevsky *The Possessed* (2004), a hero describes an epileptic aura: "During those five seconds I lived through a lifetime, and for them, I would give away my whole life because it's worth it." These experiences are so far removed from the lives of the vast majority of people that, I suspect, many regard them as a product of Dostoyevsky's imagination. Many people do not know that very similar experiences occur all the time, though perhaps in more mundane settings.

Fyodor Dostoyevsky was an epileptic who turned his "sacred disease" into brilliant writing. (Adobe collection).

The research that has been conducted to gain insight into this subject concerns mainly temporal lobe epilepsies. Researchers who study this type of epilepsy report that mystical experiences associated with it are remarkably common. Out of 69 patients analysed in one study, 26 were found to be preoccupied with religious ideas. Before the onset of their illness, *only eight* patients had religious interests[c] (Dewhurst & Beard, 1970, pp. 497–507). Some of the epilepsy-provoked conversion experiences were quite dramatic. A bus driver who had been demoted to the conductor as a result of his epileptic predisposition had, during one of his trips, a feeling of profound bliss. He collected the fares correctly, telling his passengers at the same time how pleased he was to be in Heaven. He told his G.P. later that at first, he felt "as if a bomb had burst in his head." The patient was examined in a hospital, and a possibility of degeneration in the right temporal lobe was indicated. Some years later this patient had another revelation experience, which convinced him that the ideas of Heaven and Hell were unreal and that Christ could not possibly have been conceived in any other manner except by his mother and father. The second revelation, like the first, brought to him a sense of joy, well-being and clarity of mind.

Another patient had a vision of flying in an airplane over some mountains in France. Then the aircraft climbed higher and brought him into "a land of peace," he had no cares or burdens and felt the power of God upon him. When discharged from a hospital, the patient attended a talk at a Billy Graham meeting and became a committed member of the Pentecostal Church. He used to walk the streets with a banner saying, "Be prepared to meet thy God," and acquired a tendency to bring any conversation around to a religious topic. An even more dramatic conversion happened to a patient who began having epileptic fits at the age of seventeen. At 33 he stopped taking anticonvulsants, and the frequency of his fits increased. Around this time, "he

---

[c] Two British researchers, Kenneth Dewhurst and A. W. Beard have conducted a detailed survey, linking contemporary and historical cases of the temporal lobe epilepsy with religious conversion experiences. These and the following quotes and data are from their study.

suddenly realized that he was the Son of God; he possessed special powers of healing and could abolish cancer from the world; he had visions and believed that he could understand other people's thoughts." During the following five years he felt himself as if operated by some higher power (which he variously termed as "God" and "electrical power") and communicated with his dead father and with God.

These contemporary cases have some well-known historical precedents. The conversion of St Paul is often quoted. The incident on the road to Damascus involved falling down, hearing voices, seeing things, and experiencing temporary blindness. More information is available in the case of another Christian mystic – St Teresa of Avila (1515-1582), (Avila, 2005, pp. 230-234). As noted by her biographer, she experienced visions, suffered from chronic headaches and had temporary lapses of consciousness. When she was young, she reported seeing diabolical apparitions, and at the age of 24, she fell into a coma and was considered dead. Upon recovery her tongue was found to be bitten, her joints strained, and her body covered in bruises. She later related that there were constant noises in her head: "a number of rushing waterfalls within my brain; while in other parts, drowned by the noise of the water, are the noises of birds singing and whistling." This sort of phenomena is usually caused by some pathological process in the temporal lobe – a part of the brain that is intimately involved in auditory experiences.

Another famous mystic, St Therese of Lisieux (1873-1897), (Thérèse & Edmonson, 2006), began to have experiences resembling temporal lobe epilepsy when she was about nine years old. There were "strange and violent tremblings all over her body" from which she thought she was going to die. She suffered from terrifying hallucinations, which gradually changed to visions of a religious nature. In Florence another saint, St Catherine de Ricci (1522-1590) had visual hallucinations, suffered from stigmata, and regularly lost consciousness for prolonged periods of time. Other Christian mystics are also included because of the symptoms which accompanied their religious experiences: Saint Catherine of Genoa (1447-1510), Madame Guyon (1648-1717) and Saint Marguerite Marie (1647-1690). Manifested symptoms: sensations of extremes of hot and cold trembling of the whole body, transient aphasia, automatism, passivity feelings, hyperaesthesia, childish regression, dissociation, somnambulism, transient paresis, increased suggestibility and an inability to open the eyes.[d]

One can, of course, object to this linking of mystical experience with epileptic conditions by saying: but could not these experiences, no matter what their physical manifestations, be of "higher" origin? They may be superficially similar to certain pathological conditions, but surely there is much more to it than that! This argument can, of course, be reversed. Why is it that these "higher" states had to manifest themselves through conditions identical to those linked with established cases of clinical epilepsy? Naturally, the elaboration upon their experiences is going to differ between the case of a Dostoyevsky and the case of some semi-literate bus driver. Most of the traditional mystics whose histories were recorded for us were quite remarkable individuals in their own right. Thousands of other mystical people with epilepsy must have vanished without a trace, even though their subjective experiences may have been no less powerful than those of Saint Paul or Dostoyevsky. They were unable to

---

[d] Aphasia – impairment or loss of speech; hyperaesthesia - heightened sensitivity to pain, heat, cold, etc.; paresis – loss of muscular power but not the sensation in partial paralysis.

express them and utilize them to their full capacity; it is only natural that sensations of peace and blissfulness of an unusual intensity would be, in most people's minds, readily converted into the customary notions of heaven or heavenly tranquillity.

Many people are unaware that stimulation of various other brain centres is capable of evoking extremely unusual and complex sensations.

When Penfield (2015) found that stimulation of certain parts of the human brain was making his patients perceive whole strands of memory in an orderly fashion, it caught him completely by surprise. This was despite the fact that by then there was voluminous literature on the symptoms accompanying epileptic fits. Even though the irritation in his patients' brains was due to some small physical lesions, the symptoms manifested themselves as rather complex mental states. Feelings of persecution, fear, the anticipation of some disaster, desire to be alone, overwhelming sadness, feelings of familiarity or estrangement, and even feelings of "unnecessariness" – these are some of the symptoms found in descriptions of temporal lobe epilepsy.

It makes one think that in our brain there are locations in which we have various ordinary sensations contained in their pure form. These various sensations will be "fed in," in a diluted form, to give our perceptions their familiar or unfamiliar, pleasant or unpleasant, real or unreal, necessary or unnecessary quality. It is hard to see how one can otherwise explain the presence of these pure undiluted sensations in epilepsy, in mystical states and during artificial stimulation of the brain. *The similarities between epileptic and mystical experiences are often quite striking.* There is, for example, an aura of "depersonalization" which makes the individual feel estranged from himself and his surroundings while watching them as if from outside. This feeling is very close to the mystical experiences of total "detachment."

It is also known that these and similar experiences sometimes accompany the administration of hallucinogenic drugs which, obviously, affect not messages from higher planes of existence, but neurotransmitter messages. Of course, one can conveniently envisage that God, in His wisdom, has provided us with two *identical* sets of neural ganglia, one of which is to provide us with mystical experiences of the profane and the other one of the sacred variety (Zaehner, 1978 & 1989). Presumably, only those that are destined to pursue traditional religious paths (and particularly those who belong to whatever creed we ourselves happen to subscribe) are providently endowed with the neural equipment suitable for "proper" transcendence. Those who get off on wrong tangents (no matter how similar their experiences might be to the "sacred" variety), may be sick, are deluding themselves or are prey to tricks of imagination.

There is a description of one state, also caused by an epileptic irritation, which I find almost disconcerting. A patient, described by Paul MacLean (MacLean, 1990), had an epileptic condition (with a focus in the left medial temporal region), which was preceded by a vivid sensation of "knowing the absolute truth." As the patient says, "Each time this happens, thoughts occur very clear and bright to me...as if this is what the world is all about...[this is] the absolute truth." As MacLean (1973, p. 8) summarizes:

"Here is evidence that a primitive system of our brain that *represents an inheritance from lower mammals* (my italics) is able to generate, all out of context, a feeling of what is real, true, and important."

Dostoyevsky in *Idiot* also mentions an epileptic aura that provided a sensation of "existence in the most intense degree" (2016). I suppose this is about as far as one can go in localizing "pure" aspects of our ordinarily diluted and intermingled perceptions of reality. Apparently, the perception of these intense varieties of ordinary sensations out of context is not confined to cases of clear-cut pathology or recognized mysticism. In one national survey conducted in the U.S., 29% of all people asked reported having déjà vu experiences at least once or twice in their lives, and 6% had them often (Greeley, 1974, p. 139).

The tapping of these ordinarily subconscious reservoirs of powerful sensations contained in the limbic structures might, in some cases, bring a subjective feeling of expanded awareness and greater clarity. The importance of the subconscious in a creative act has often been emphasized. It is known for example that the German chemist August Kekule discovered the formula of the benzine ring on the basis of a dream he had. Henri Poincaré, the French mathematician, could not solve a certain difficult mathematical problem by conscious effort but came to a creative insight while taking a walk by the seaside. However, a lot of conscious exploration usually occurs before the subconscious creative insight can take place. It is true that Charles Darwin discovered his theory of evolution while taking a ride in a carriage but this would have been hardly possible had he not spent many years gathering and evaluating masses of the biological specimen and sifting of evolutionary ideas (Crow, 1971, p. 310).

Chapter 1. The "Sacred Disease" and Other Paranormal States | 31

"**What's it all about?**" (Fiantsev, 2017b)

Dostoyevsky gives us a glimpse of the productive, creative potentialities felt by person with an epilepsy in *Idiot*:

There was one stage right before the attack (if it happened when one was awake) when, all of a sudden, right in the midst of sadness, spiritual darkness and depression, his brain was momentary as if set aflame and his whole life force enlivened to an unusual degree. The sensation of living and of being conscious would increase nearly tenfold during these lightning-like moments. His mind, his heart would become aglow with an extraordinary light; all his doubts, all troubles would suddenly subside and resolve themselves into some higher quietude, which was full of transparent, harmonious joy and hope, full of wisdom and total understanding (Dostoyevsky, 2016).

But all of this was only a prelude to that final "unbearable moment" of the appreciation of "the highest synthesis of life." It is interesting that here Dostoyevsky, speaking through the words of one of his heroes, also draws a line between these supposedly sacred revelations and the profane stupefying influences of "hashish, opium, and wine."

We realize that the potentialities so lucidly described by Dostoyevsky do not automatically flow out of a transcendent state when we compare his case with that of the epileptic bus driver, quoted earlier. He also had a vivid subjective feeling that his mind was "cleared." However, when he put down his religious ideas in a letter to his wife, they turned out to be completely unintelligible.

This is an appropriate moment to remind the reader that we have been talking only about a relatively small number of epileptic cases. Even among the temporal lobe epileptics, only about a quarter become *newly* preoccupied with religious ideas, and out of those, only a third did have vivid conversion experiences. This comprises about 5% of all epileptic cases, which is probably an overestimate. This would mean that in a nation of 200,000,000 people, about 50,000 people might have undergone religious conversion as a result of temporal lobe epilepsy (it is considered that, on the average, one person in 200 suffers from epilepsy).

In most cases, auras consist of unpleasant odours or tastes, fear, peculiar gastric sensations, and/or various auditory and visual distortions. The attacks usually leave a person in a shattered state and, with frequent repetition, may lead to the more general physical and psychological disorders. I doubt if even Dostoyevsky himself quite meant it when he spoke about giving his whole life away for one moment of his aura. It is hard to say whether he would have been taking anti-convulsants had he lived in our times. He had of course sincerely believed that he, like Mohammed, really visited Heaven in those moments. But he also had his reservations. He spoke of dullness, mental turbidity, and debility, which were the inevitable consequence of these "higher moments."

II. In the Beginning, there was the Rhythm

Beginning in 1946, W. Grey Walter, one of the pioneers in the field of electrical studies of brain activity, found that epilepsy-like phenomena could be experimentally produced in entirely normal subjects. At the end of the war, Grey Walter and his collaborators began to use bright flashes of a strobe light in conjunction with EEG (brain wave pattern) recordings (Banquet, 1973, 449). The rate of flashing could be regulated by turning a knob. It was found that at certain very precise frequencies (e.g. not 9, or 10.5, but exactly 10 flashes per second), the electrical potentials evoked in the brain of the experimental subject by rhythmically flashing light were spilling over across the usually impassable borders in the brain. The flashing *light* might, for example, provoke a ringing sensation in the subject's *ears*, thus breaking down physiological barriers between the visual and the auditory regions of the brain. This is precisely the mechanism underlying most forms of epilepsy: a strong impulse originating in some area of the brain tends to spread around and involve greater and greater numbers of neurons, which would ordinarily not take part in a synchronous discharge.

Grey Walter (1963, p. 92) and his collaborators wanted to see what percentage of the normal subjects would respond to the flicker. They tested several hundred people who came from all walks of life and who had never had an epileptic fit. In 3-4% of all cases tested, scientists were able to find the frequency that triggered responses similar to those found in epileptic subjects. When the right frequency was achieved, people would report "strange feelings," "swimming in the head," faintness, and even brief periods of unconsciousness. Some jerked their limbs in synchrony with the flashing light; some reported sensations of "tingling," etc. As soon as these responses occurred, the flicker was turned off. This technique proved that epilepsy-like symptoms could be produced in completely normal subjects. We must remember that the general incidence of epilepsy among the population is only 0.5%, which is significantly lower than the percentage reported by Walter.

Later, a more sophisticated flicker apparatus was constructed. It had a built-in triggering mechanism, which fired the flicker in synchrony with brainwaves. A feedback system was devised to keep the flicker and the constantly fluctuating brainwave pattern in tune. With this piece of equipment, Walter writes: "In more than 50% of young normal adult subjects, the first exposure to feedback flicker evokes transient paroxysmal discharges of the type seen so often in epileptics" (Walter, 1963, p. 92).

These observations are backed up by reports of epilepsy-like phenomena that sometimes occur in perfectly normal people and under natural circumstances in response to flickering light. Walter quotes a case in which a person experienced a violent jerk as he was being driven through a forest with the sun flickering through the trees. Another curious case concerns a cyclist who nearly "passed out" a few times as he was cycling in the forest with the sun's rays flickering through the trees. A temporary loss of control would make him slow down and bring the frequency below its effective range. This would terminate the dimming of consciousness. Yet another person found that the flickering on a movie screen was provoking violent impulses and dimmed consciousness in him. When tested in the laboratory, he developed powerful jerking of the limbs when the frequency of stimulation was brought up to about 50 flashes per second – which approximates the flicker rate of a movie projector.

One can compare the mechanism by which rhythmic stimulation breaks down barriers between different regions of the brain with the well-known cases of powerful reverberations produced, for example, by a platoon of soldiers marching in step across a bridge. If they continue to march in step and reinforce the vibration, the structure of the bridge is affected and may even collapse. This is the reason why marching columns are allowed to break the step when passing over a bridge. The kind of feedback flicker described above is capable of producing an even more perfectly synchronized oscillation of brain rhythms. After a certain point, the oscillation becomes too powerful to be contained within one brain structure and starts to spill beyond the normal physiological pathways in the brain. With people who are predisposed to epilepsy, these runaway oscillations can be produced relatively easily. With them, a flickering picture on the television screen, to give one example, may be enough to provoke an epileptic fit. In fact, specialists regard television as one of the worst offenders in children's epilepsy.[e] Not only the fragmentary sensations already described, but also complete and organized hallucination-like feelings involving more than one sense were provoked by flicker stimulation (Miller, 1961, pp. 387-397).

Not only visual but also other types of rhythmic stimulation were shown to initiate the spill-over processes in the human brain. This was done with the use of a rhythmic clicking sound. The effective frequency of stimulation was similar to visual precipitation, even though different brain rhythms and receptor structures were involved. The frequency of visual flicker stimulation was usually in the range of 10 to 20 per second and for auditory – less than 30 per second. In support of these findings, cases of "musicogenic epilepsy" (epilepsy caused by exposure to music) are sometimes reported in the literature. In many cases, only classical music or music with a strong rhythm seems to be effective. Sometimes the emotional associations provoked by music ("sad," "sentimental") appeared to play a role. Even cases of epileptic precipitation by church bells (Dostoyevsky) were reported. The effective frequencies, in

---

[e] There are also reports of the existence of a crowd dispersal device incorporating an extremely bright strobe light flushing frequencies at certain predetermined sequences.

this case, were found to be in a band between 290 and 1120 cycles per second.

We can now take a closer look at the anatomical structures that may be involved in some of the experiences described above. It has been noticed that some people subjected to flicker stimulation experienced feelings of fatigue, confusion, disgust, anger and pleasure. It is natural to assume that, in these cases, the discharge involved various structures in the limbic system, which have been shown to regulate these various emotional states. We also know that the temporal lobe and the limbic system are located close to each other and are interconnected. Involvement of the limbic system is also indicated by the fact that emotional upsets and particularly fear are some of the most common triggers of epilepsy. Even in animals, a sudden loud noise may precipitate something like an epileptic fit. Specialists have grouped these epilepsies under the title of "startle" epilepsies. One investigator emphasizes that the fear, which an epileptic feels, is not fear of something in particular, but "fear which comes by itself – the symptom fear" (in other words, "pure" fear), (Merlis, 1974, pp. 440-456).

An even clearer connection between many epileptic disorders and the limbic system is indicated by the fact that the sense of smell is often involved. Smell is one of the most "limbic" senses (as pointed out earlier, the limbic lobe used to be called the "smell-brain" and was supposed to deal primarily with smell perception). The capacity of certain pungent smells to elicit fits in people with epilepsy was well known throughout the ages. An old poem, attributed to a mythical Greek hero Orpheus (Orpheus, 2015), describes how burning jet (black mineral, resembling coal) affects epileptics:

> Jet too he flees, which through ascending vapors
> All mortals makes to suffer with its pungency
> Smoke-hued and flat, not large to look upon,
> It flames up brightly like some dried up fir,
> Yet to the nostrils brings destructive power; and man
> Will not escape the test thou settest
> To prove them sufferers from the sacred ill.
> For quickly will they bend and forward tilt,
> As to the earth it draws them. Smeared by froth
> From their own mouths, hither and thither will they turn,
> And wallow on the ground.

The belief that strong odours can trigger epilepsy was so widespread that slaves used to be tested for potential epilepsy by exposure to burning jet. The ancient physicians were also not too far behind the achievements of modern experimental physiology: they used to test predisposition to epilepsy by exposure to a light flickering through a potter's wheel. Epileptics were advised by their physicians to avoid looking at turning wheels of carriages in the street. The physiological mechanism, which underlies the influence of odours on an epileptic, was most elegantly, if not sufficiently scientifically, summed up by the Aristotelian philosopher Alexander of Aphrodisias (2012):

> For the thickness of the particles of the odours carried up through the nose, thickens and condenses the psychic pneuma, which is already thick and cold, and renders the psychic pneuma unfit for functions of the soul. Now the body, if not supported by the soul, is overcome by its own weight and falls down.

Another Greek physician, Arotaeus the Cappadocian (Kotsopoulos, 1986, pp. 171-179), had with great acuity pinpointed symptoms all of which are indicative of the limbic system involvement: "The patients feel their ears ringing [temporal lobe], they smell bad odours ["smell-brain"], are irritable and become angry without reason" [limbic structures such as amygdala, which were shown to provoke anger experimentally]."

Nowadays, the importance of odours in precipitating epilepsy is played down. Some experiments prove, however, that the electrical activity of the temporal lobe shows spike discharges characteristic of epilepsy when people are exposed to perfumed air. The peculiar odours frequently reported by epileptics as part of their auras are probably internally produced. In other words, they result from the excitation of neurons in the smell-regulating areas in the brain itself and therefore represent one more example of a "pure" undiluted sensation. Typical is the case of an epileptic patient described earlier (the "Son of God" case) who told his doctors that he could perceive a "holy smell." Usually, the smells reported by people with epilepsy are, however, unpleasant and difficult to describe. It has already been mentioned that the sense of smell is located in the brain in close proximity to the centres that regulate sexual functions. This is due to the importance placed upon the sense of smell in the sexual repertoire of mammals from which we evolved. The areas that produce pleasure in intracranial stimulation (septum and medial forebrain bundle) are also intimately interconnected with the olfactory bulb.

We may summarize by saying that in the case of epileptics, as well as in normal subjects in experimental and natural settings, a rhythmic stimulation of a particular

frequency may break down normal physiological barriers between different regions of the brain. When this happens, people become aware of such sensations as intense pleasure or pain or peculiar sensations ordinarily associated with mystical experiences. These sensations can be traced down to certain limbic structures whose involvement is supported by the influence of smell and emotional excitement upon precipitation of an epileptic fit.

III. But what do I love, when I love Thee?

We can observe milder versions of the phenomena discussed not only in cases of confirmed epilepsy or in an experimental laboratory, but in everyday life. Marghanita Laski's book *Ecstasy* (1961) contains descriptions and analyses of ecstatic experiences reported in the literature and in response to her own questionnaire data. Laski makes it very clear that the experiences recorded by her have nothing to do with any "morbid conditions" and that they presumably emanate from some higher realm of the human psyche. She quotes approvingly a memorable passage from William James (1971, p. 35) *The Varieties of Religious Experience*.

> Medical materialism finishes up St. Paul by calling his vision on the road to Damascus a discharging lesion of the occipital cortex, he being an epileptic. It snuffs out St. Theresa as a hysteric, St. Francis of Assisi as a hereditary degenerate. George Fox's discontent with the shams of his age, and his pining for spiritual veracity; it treats as a symptom of a disordered colon. Carlyle's organ tones of

misery it accounts for by a gastro-duodenal catarrh (James, 2013).

The question of normality or otherwise of these experiences will be dealt with at the end of this chapter. First, we must try to look objectively at the exact neurological circumstances that provoke such ecstatic experiences as described by Laski.

One is tempted immediately to recognize some experiences as fairly straightforward descriptions of psychological phenomena that accompany some epileptic fits:

This ecstasy lasted from half an hour to an hour, and whether his souls were in the body, or out of the body, he could not tell. But when he came to his senses it seemed to him that he returned from another world. And so greatly did his body suffer in this short rupture that it seemed to him that none, even in dying, could suffer so greatly in so short time. The Servitor came to himself moaning, and he fell down upon the ground like a man who swoons and he cried inwardly heaving great sighs from the depths of his soul and saying, 'Oh, my God, where was I and where am I?' And again, 'Oh, my heart's joy, never shall my soul forget this hour!' He walked but it was, but his body that walked, as a machine may do (Laski, 1961).

Some other experiences, such as that of Tennyson ("thick night came down upon my eyelids, and I fell") are also suggestive of epilepsy. However, one can argue endlessly, especially in the cases of historical personalities, about whether we are dealing with epileptic phenomena or ambiguous descriptions. We should look not so much at isolated incidents as at the whole spectrum presented by these experiences.

What were the most frequent triggers of the ecstatic experiences reported by Laski's correspondents? Music is mentioned more often than any other art stimulus. Another frequent trigger is flickering light or flashes of light. Sounds familiar? Here are some of the key phrases describing circumstances that acted as triggers: "When the light and the smell and the scene is just right;" "the newly-risen sun sent flickering...a series of elastic reflections;" "the shining waters glittering in my dreamy eyes;" "flickering red flames;" "the lights of the sun shining on the metal of the cars was dazzling." There is also flickering on the water, which seems to flash *through the body* of the person describing his experiences; sunlight flickering through leaves; fires flickering in grates and flickering starlight. As Laski notes herself, "It would be possible to multiply almost indefinitely examples of sudden or flashing light appearing both in actual triggers to ecstasy and in images used to describe the feelings of ecstasy." There are also feelings of "thrills, shudders, and tingling" associated with the flashes. Laski attributes all this to the possible effects of atmospheric electricity during stormy weather.

Two people mentioned in Laski's book even had their epileptic experiences triggered by a film. Another frequent trigger mechanism was "regular rhythmic movement." An authority on art and inspiration, quoted by Laski, explains this connection:

> It is possible that the rhythmic movement of a carriage or train, or a horse and to a much lesser degree of walking may produce on sensitive minds a slightly hypnotic

effect conducive to that state of mind most favourable to the birth of ideas.

It is also extremely interesting that among "literary" triggers there were mostly poetic works (endowed with rhythm and emotion), fiction being mentioned only by one person. "Scent – the odour of flowers, trees, the earth, etc.," writes Laski, "is often mentioned in accounts of trigger circumstances." In one particular case, the smell was reported as the only trigger. Another person writes that after his experience, "All creation gave another smell unto me than before." "Can scent to any extent act as an intoxicant in inducing ecstasy?" wonders Laski.

Some of Laski's correspondents reported feelings which were strikingly similar to those found in limbic epilepsy. There are for example, "dreamy mental states" and feelings of "having been here before" (*dèjá vu*). There are various other sensations reported, some of which resemble epileptic auras. There is a "terrific constriction in the throat and stomach," "something... inflating my entire being," etc. Experiences of refined breathing and peace are also very common. People spoke of a "standstill feeling," a "complete calm," a "tranquil ecstasy." Laski was surprised that so many people reported negative or mixed feelings together with ecstatic ones. Others spoke of "sadness mixed with joy," "disturbing presence," "great agony...and terror," "a violent throb of emotion." This is perhaps less surprising if one keeps in mind the close anatomical proximity of the structures which mediate pleasure and pain. An uncontrolled discharge brought about by rhythmic stimulation may spread across the boundaries and involve both of these areas, producing "mixed" feelings.

Furthermore, a connection between ecstatic feelings and basic drives, such as hunger or sex, was sometimes mentioned. In two cases ecstatic feelings were actually provoked by eating pleasant foods. More tenuous – some would say only metaphorical – connection, as well as differentiation, between basic needs and their ecstatic counterparts, can be inferred from St. Augustine's description of religious ecstasy:

> But what do I love, when I love thee? Not beauty of bodies, nor the fair harmony of time, not the brightness of the light, so gladsome to our eyes, nor sweet melodies of varied songs, nor the fragrant smell of flowers, and ointments, and spices, nor manna and honey, nor limbs acceptable to embracement of flesh. None of these I love, when I love my God; and yet I love a kind of light, and melody, and fragrance, and meat, and embracement, when I love my God, the light, melody, fragrance, meat, embracement of my inner man; where there shineth unto my soul, what space cannot contain, and there soundeth, what time beareth not away, and there smelleth, what breathing disperses not, and there tasteth, what eating diminisheth not, and there clingeth, what satiety divorceth not (Laski, 1961).

Here one finds an eloquent confirmation from no lesser authority on mystic's psychology than St. Augustine (2012) that ultimate rewards are closely linked to basic drives, and yet transcend them in some way.

As could well be expected, some people connected their ecstatic experiences directly with sex, while others expressed their feelings through similes full of sexual overtones. It is interesting to note in this connection that Kinsey reported in his investigation of sexual practices that one out of every six pre-adolescent boys and a small proportion of men sometimes experienced violent convulsions during and after orgasm. All ancient authorities, almost without exception, elaborated upon the close connection between sex and epilepsy. Most often, sexual activities were supposed to aggravate epilepsy.

Only very rarely was sex regarded as a cure. It was noticed that many epileptic disorders disappear around the age of puberty; if they continued after that, the prognosis was considered much worse. Some contemporary investigators also point out the connection between epilepsy and the level of sex hormones in patients' blood. Inferring cause and effect relationship between the onset of puberty and the disappearance of epilepsy, some ancient physicians even "did violence to the nature of children by unseasonable coition" to effect an early cure. This permissive attitude was rather exceptional and most attempts to cure epilepsy by alteration of sexual behaviour centred around, as befits general attitudes of those days, such things as enforced abstinence and, occasionally, castration or clitoridectomy.

This tradition of confusion between the sacred and the sexual is indeed a time-honoured one. At the ancient Anatolian town of Catal Huyuk (circa 6000 BC) we find some of the earliest Neolithic representations of the *hieros gamos*, the "sacred marriage," depicting two deities locked in a tight embrace. The phallic festivals of Egyptians, the Dionysiac celebrations of ancient Greeks, the Saturnalias of Romans, the sexual frenzy of Russian Khlysty (the Whips) – all bear testimony to the recognition of the significant overlap between man's highest aspirations of religious transcendence and the supposedly lowest "animalistic" drives.

An even more significant confirmation of this overlap comes from those who have actually had the "peak experience" towards which all mystics strive (Steuart, 1999).

> Oh, night that was my guide!
> Oh darkness dearer than the morning's pride,
> Oh night that joined the lover
> To the beloved bride
> Transfiguring them into each other.

What is this? The ravings of a Cupid-struck honeymooner? The sublimated longings of some second-rate poet of the Age or Romance? No, these are the words of the celebrated Christian mystic, St. John of the Cross, trying his best to describe his union with the Divine in our limited earthly vocabulary (Steuart, 1999).

"Let me do my pleasure," he said. "There is a time for everything. Now I want you to be the plaything of my love, and you must live thus without resistance, surrendering to my desires, allowing me to gratify myself at your expense."

Thus does another saint, St. Mary Margaret Alacogue (1986) express her vision of God speaking to her like a seductive and demanding Casanova.

Some mystics describe the actual experience of transcendence in terms that denote sensations suspiciously orgasmic in nature. St. Teresa of Avila (2005, pp. 230-234) speaks of vision in which an angel came to her with a long and fire-tipped golden spear, which he repeatedly "plunged... into my deepest inward. When he drew it out, I thought my entrails would be drawn out too, and when he left me, I glowed in the hot fire of love for God. The pain was so strong that I screamed aloud but simultaneously felt such infinite sweetness that I wished the pain to last forever. It was the sweetest caressing of the soul by God." Many contemporary men's magazines would kill for writing like this.

St. Francis of Sales (Fedorchek, 2007) speaks of religious rapture in terms which are also suggestive:

> ...as melted balm that no longer has firmness or solidity the soul lets herself pass or flow into what she loves... The outflow of a soul into her God is a true ecstasy by which the soul transcends the limits of her natural way of existence, being totally mingled and engulfed in, her God.

The nature of the "communion with the Divine" also assumed frankly physical connotations in some forms of American Revivalism, where converts were sometimes deliberately encouraged to "come through" to Jesus, this being considered a sign of God's grace.

As reported by Laski (1961), sexual love appeared to be a frequent trigger of mystical experiences, mentioned by nearly half of the people surveyed by her. Some of them made quite explicit references to sexual intercourse, while others alluded to it in a more oblique fashion. Laski herself, in common with other religiously inclined commentators, tries to separate somehow the mystical and the erotic. One of her chief arguments is as follows: The religious mystics usually assume a passive female role in their love relationship with God; "In sexual intercourse," writes Laski defiantly, "whether ecstatic or not, no male, so far as I know, feels himself to be playing the part of the female and his female that of a male." No comment.

However, is there any real reason to suppose that the mystical and the erotic are connected in more than a purely accidental fashion? If we look at the diagram of the human brain, we see a picture that strangely upsets our understanding of the geography of the human body. In the brain, our mouths and our genitals (as well as our anuses) are not separated by the respectful distances which we tend to regard as being God-given but are actually crowded into one tightly interconnected neural ring. As Paul MacLean (1990) wryly observed, "Civilized man long suspected that the world was round before Columbus sailed to America, but how could they have imagined that the limbic lobe [our animal brain] was a closed ring and that in voyaging in one direction the head would be reached by the way of the tail and vice versa." The centres of pleasure, sex, fighting, and hunger all lie in this innermost part of our brain in close proximity. No wonder that confusion between some of these areas arises (Stanley-Jones, 1970, pp. 25-37).

In the same ancient part of the brain, there are also sites that, when excited during epilepsy or electrical brain stimulation, provoke sensations indistinguishable from those reported by religious mystics. The pieces of the jigsaw puzzle with the seemingly incongruous pictures of embracing gods and epileptic saints and Secrets of the Universe begin to fit together surprisingly well. Yet, can we unreservedly equate transcendental bliss experienced by a mystic to a purely sexual orgasm? There must be some fire behind the smoke, some truth in the unanimous observation by recognized mystics that their "spiritual marriage" is of a different order than the mundane sexuality of their lay brethren. What is it, if anything at all, that makes the "fragrance, meat, and embracement" of St. Augustine and other mystics different from our own fleshy variety?

Could it be that it is the breathlessness, the "peace that passeth all understanding," the "oceanic feeling," the "tranquil ecstasy," the "standstill feeling" that differentiates the two types of experiences? Certainly, the emphasis on complete passivity is one of the most frequently encountered components of a profound mystical experience. Usually, the pleasant feelings which we experience while listening to music, for example, or after having a good meal or intercourse or both are associated with a passive state of mind and body. Sexual orgasm represents one of the very few exceptions where Nature was obliged, so to speak, to reward us generously even though we were in a state of extremely vigorous activity. Here, a neurological compromise had to be struck because of the tremendous importance of fighting behaviour as a preliminary to mating. No wonder orgasm resembles an epileptic fit! Now if we could tap the same reservoir of pleasure but in a passive state, the rewards would be so much greater. Thus, another piece of the jigsaw puzzle falls into place: the bliss that the mystic experience is derived from the same source as the one which is tapped to reinforce sexual and other drives, only its quantity and quality are vastly different due to the state of extreme passivity in which the mystic receives his Heavenly Reward.

Santa Maria. (Adobe collection).

Ignorance of the physiological discrepancy between the orgasm and transcendental ecstasy led to a tremendous amount of confusion among the seekers of "heavenly rewards." The follower of the sexual practices of Tantric yoga (or the sex-orientated follower of the Occult) could not overlook the obvious connection between the transcendent and the erotic and decided to reach the former through exaggerated emphasis upon the latter. The ascetic, on the contrary, discerned the superior nature of transcendental bliss and decided to reach it through suppression of carnal desires. In reality, as we can see, the profound mystical experience is only indirectly connected with the sexual drive and can co-exist, barring excesses, with either sexual activity or its absence in the same way that it can co-exist with relative satiety or hunger. As we shall see, either the suppression of sexual desire or its excessive promotion will, if anything, hamper the arrival of a profound mystical experience.

The sexual rites of either Tantrism or the Occult almost invariably seem to lead us to the deep chasms of what even the most liberated will be obliged to call perversions. In certain Tantric practices, the devotees are required to perform necrophilic (corpse-defiling) rites at cemeteries. To inspire a suitable amount of terror, which is deemed to be necessary for the attainment of success in subsequent practices, the practitioners of Tantric rites are required to contemplate the destructive aspects of Siva as a black-limbed, wrathful being, accompanied by ghouls, demons and ogresses. Hashish is often taken before the ritual intercourse, which is then performed by a number of couples sitting in a circle. While this is going on, sacred mantras are chanted. A great deal of fuss is made of semen discharge, which is either eliminated or is meticulously collected and reabsorbed (through the mouth) to prevent the loss of this magical substance.

In a well-documented case of the occultist Aleister Crowley, ritual intercourse was usually performed until complete exhaustion was achieved. Any means whatsoever were used to obtain further orgasms. Homosexual intercourse, sadistic mutilation, drinking of semen mixed with menstrual blood, etc., were practised. There is no doubt that these practices could produce an altered state of consciousness (Crowley used to affectionately label it "Eroto-comatose Lucidity"). There can also be little doubt that they are severely detrimental to the physical and psychological wellbeing of the person who practises them. Crowley himself died a ruined man, hopelessly addicted to heroin.

Let us now look at what the Ascetic Path has to offer. The history of ascetic, practices is almost too well known to need further elucidation. Some gems, however, bear recapitulation. One of them is a yogic practice called Vajroli Mudra, aimed at achieving the state of Brahmacharya (sexual celibacy in this context). It entails drawing into one's urethra first milk, then honey, then *mercury*!

An eyewitness at one of the penitent festivals in India describes the following practices:

> Every inch of one man's body was pierced with small hooks...A few naked women had arrows penetrating their breasts, stomachs and buttocks so that they could neither sit nor lie down... A woman was hanging from hooks attached to her breasts and vagina, the two centres of desire (Gellhorn & Loofbourrow, 1963, p. 242).

It may well be that the superior rewards obtained by a few mystics made sexual satisfaction unnecessary and unattractive to them. We know from experimentation with animals that pleasure centre activation makes them, at least for a while, oblivious to the "worldly pleasures" of sex and food. However, some recent long-term experiments have shown that after the novelty of the experience wears off, these experimental animals begin to incorporate direct brain stimulation into their normal routine, alternating it with sex and food intake. In another interesting experiment by two Swedish researchers, the mating behaviour of 15 male albino rats was shown to be unrelated to direct brain stimulation. The rats naturally preferred to self-stimulate, rather than copulate, but the frequency of their mating and the rate of self-stimulation were not related to each other in any meaningful manner (Karlsson & Larsson, 1975, pp. 7–10).

What can we infer from all this qualitative and experimental evidence pertaining to tantric sex, occultists, and ascetics? Most significantly, I think, we can take it as a case study on the effects of "extreme" behaviour on the mind. In many cases, both human and animal, it is easy to see how stimulation of the brain via either extreme indulgence or extreme denial can initiate the so-called mystical experiences. However, the long-term results of the various rat experiments in the previous paragraph also indicate that most organisms tend to fall within the "normal" range of behaviour even when receiving regular brain stimulation.

IV. The Inside out of Abnormality

We have finally come to the whole question of "normality" or "abnormality" of the experiences discussed. I realize that the analysis presented above can be taken to prove the supposed morbidity of certain spiritual experiences. However, it may just as well serve as an indication of "normality" of some supposedly pathological conditions. In many cases, the dividing line is supplied by our emotional prejudices and by cultural norms and is therefore practically meaningless. But let us take a closer look at this dividing line in relation to epilepsy.

As already pointed out, it is possible, with the aid of a specially constructed apparatus, to induce epilepsy-like states in 50% of all people who have never had any epileptic fits and will probably never have one. An injection of sub-convulsant doses of the drug Metrazol (which raises the level of excitability of brain cells and therefore facilitates the spread of neural discharges) prior even to a crude version of the flicker test can provoke epileptic jerks (myoclonic epilepsy) in any perfectly normal individual and, if the stimulation is continued, precipitate a full-scale seizure.

Some authorities state quite emphatically that, in principle, epilepsy is not a disease but a syndrome, something some people have more of than others do. A well-known and respected neurologist W. Ritchie Russel writes: "In most respects the brain of the epileptic and of the normal person are alike, but the one is more easily forced into convulsions than the other." (Russel, 1959, p. 91). W. Grey Walter also regards epilepsy as a natural phenomenon (and *not* a degenerative disease) that may occur whenever a very large number of nervous cells are clustered together. He says, "When we have enough data... we may get a statistical answer indicating to what extent epileptic seizures may be a necessity for this or that degree of complexity of combination between the myriad million units of our Olympian nerve-net." In other words, epilepsy is a condition that goes together with a large brain. Grey Walter even hints at the possibility that our coming down to the ground in the primeval jungle may have been due to the frequency of epileptic fits to which the swelling brains of our arboreal cousins became prone!

It is doubtful that this was the case, for the forces of natural selection would have quickly weeded out individuals who would have had a predisposition to epilepsy, which, as might well be imagined, would have been somewhat dangerous to a tree-dwelling species. However, perhaps our brains only began to grow as rapidly as they did *after* we had descended to the ground and could, therefore, remain unconscious for a few brief moments without dropping down from great heights straight into the mouths of waiting predators. A big – and epileptic – brain is a luxury only a ground-dwelling creature can afford. This is another paradox of evolution: only after being thrown out of our tropical paradise could we embark upon a brain-growing spree. The man had to fall (literally and metaphorically) to become the thinking, powerful, creative, dangerous – and unhappy, epileptic, the transcendence-seeking creature that he is.

There is a study (Walter, 1963) that proposes to view epilepsy as an evolutionary atavism (a reappearance of a characteristic belonging to a remote ancestor), which may have had something to do with adaptive behaviours of early man. Comparisons are drawn between the compulsive behaviour of a frightened deer mouse and human epilepsy. Supposedly, "playing dead" (while having an epileptic fit) could have been of survival value. An untenable explanation depicts epilepsy as a protective device against oxygen starvation to which a rapidly growing brain became prone. By falling prostrate on the ground, the oxygen supply to the brain is supposedly increased (with the limbs requiring less), and the danger of brain asphyxiation avoided.

These theories, unfortunately, ignore the difference in the degree of complexity of the human brain compared to the animal brain and a correspondingly more complex picture of epilepsy in man. We do not know of any natural counterparts to the *petit mal*, or temporal lobe fits in any wild animal. Yet it is these two varieties of fits and not the *grand mal* convulsive seizure that represents the bulk of epileptic disorders of human species. What survival value could one place on them? Two brain structures which have developed comparatively recently in man to a unique degree, the hippocampus and the lateral temporal lobe, are also frequent loci of epileptic discharges. The hippocampus in man is larger, both relatively and absolutely, than in any mammal, elephants and whales included. It is also the most unstable structure of the brain and has the lowest seizure threshold (Chance, 1963).

The hippocampus is involved in dreaming and could be linked up with both the "dreamy state" of epilepsy and schizophrenia that has been compared to a "waking dream". One of the most frequent auras – that of *déjà vu* – most probably arises in the hippocampal circuit (Green, 1964, pp. 561–608).

Between them, the temporal lobe and the hippocampus are involved in the highly complicated tasks of hearing, verbal interpretation, information retrieval and storage, and perceptual integration. It seems, therefore, that the speedy development of larger and more complex neural structures necessary for the performance of these operations was a predisposition to epilepsy. Most probably, epilepsy never had any adaptive function; it was always a liability. However, the natural selection "tolerated" this liability because greater net benefits were afforded by a growing brain. At the same time, such a widespread and debilitating imperfection of structure could only develop in a species that was not allowed to evolve at a leisurely pace. In essence, the manner and speed with which the human brain evolved left us simultaneously prone to epilepsy and relatively sheltered from many of its harmful consequences.

A simplified picture of epilepsy begins to look like this. Epileptic phenomena can be provoked by a) internal foci of excitation such as a brain tumour and b) external agents such as rhythmic stimulation, stress, fright, etc., which tend to aggravate or even cause abnormal discharges. Needless to say, genetic predisposition, imbalances of metabolic and hormonal processes, etc., can all make a person more susceptible to epilepsy. So, on the one hand, we may have a fairly straightforward case of epilepsy caused by abnormal processes (such as a head injury), while at the other extreme, we have a "normal" person who, by exposure to a multitude of loosely defined influences – hormonal, hereditary, nutritional, etc. – was made susceptible to epilepsy or epilepsy-like states. A chance combination of environmental factors – e.g. an emotionally aroused state and exposure to just the right frequency of rhythmic stimulation – may tip the balance. The mental states provoked need not at all resemble the picture of any classical epileptic fit and may have little to do with clinical epilepsy.

I have been using the term "epilepsy" because there is no other overall generic term under which we could group many of the phenomena discussed above. It would be much better to eliminate the term "epilepsy," at least for our discussion, and introduce a notion of something like a "neural cross-talk." This could be defined as the "susceptibility of brain structures to excitation and subsequent spill-over in physiologically unaccustomed directions." One can object on theoretical grounds to the use of the phrase "unaccustomed directions." For practical purposes, however, this definition will suffice. We know that something unusual is taking place when someone starts talking about a visit to Heaven after hearing the church bells ring, or when one reports that his lips feel swollen like balloons, or that he feels as if he is being "pushed sideways in time."

The high level of "cross-talk potential" (or, to coin a more familiar, if somewhat imprecise, term, the "Transcendence Quotient," abbreviated as T.Q.) is of course of fundamental importance to the possibility of having, spontaneously or otherwise, some form of "mystical" experience. But how high must it be to produce a noticeable alteration of normal awareness and what proportion of the general population could be expected to undergo its more profound varieties? We know that 3-4% of normal, healthy subjects will experience sensations resembling some symptoms of the "sacred disease," when subjected to a simple flicker test. However, only a very small minority (perhaps less than 0.1%, which is also the percentage representing the incidence of self-induced epilepsy) will experience sensations, which can, with any approximation, be called blissful. In non-laboratory situations, this percentage would be even lower, as indicated by the comparatively rare incidence of spontaneously-provoked ecstatic experiences.

There are a variety of indicators that can help one to estimate approximately one's T.Q. How often have you experienced sensations which appeared to be a strangely intensified variety of those we have normally ("having been here before," "detachment," "realness" or "unrealness" of whatever is happening, loss of identity, etc.)? Do you have frequent memory flashbacks, which vividly bring back past experiences, together with their corresponding odours, feelings, etc.? Have you experienced time distortion, false awakenings (hallucination-like dreams indistinguishable from reality), lucid dreams (dreams in which you are aware of yourself dreaming), out-of-body experiences? If you have had many of these experiences or have had them often, you are probably fairly high on the T.Q. scale.

If you are more experimentally minded, you can, at your risk, construct a portable flicker apparatus in the privacy of your home. Place a paper cylinder, with approximately 30 vertical slots cut into it, on top of a record player. Suspend a bright light bulb into the cylinder. Start the record player. This should give you, at 33 1/3 r.p.m., the average effective trigger frequency. Watch the flashing light with your eyes closed. Experiment by changing the speed or number of slots. If any unusual sensations arise, turn away from the light and stop the player.

Another useful procedure for determining the T.Q. level is the so-called eye roll test designed by the hypnotherapist Herbert Spiegel (2004). The subject is asked to roll his eyes upward as if trying to look at the top of the head. The higher the eyes roll, the greater the subject's hypnotisability (barring cases of psychopathology). There are both theoretical and practical reasons to suspect that the eye roll test may correlate positively with T.Q. Both hypnotic and mystical trance require an unusual capacity for maintaining awareness (in hypnosis, rapport) while being in a state of deep regression to a much more cortically primitive level of functioning. Normally, the upward roll of the eyes indicates loss of consciousness (in sleep, epileptic seizure, etc.). Therefore, the ability to roll the eyes upward while closing the eyelids slowly and remaining conscious may indicate a biologically in-built (the eye roll does not change throughout life and appears to be genetically determined, although the overall personality is not) capacity of the individual to maintain states of severe dissociation in his psyche. This indicator is particularly attractive because it is both quantifiable and independent of subjective volition.

It might be useful to remind the reader again that we have been mostly talking only about a particular aspect of a small number of cases where exceptionally high levels of cross-talk in a specific direction were found. A vast majority of epileptic auras, for example, comprise niggly little sensations like dizziness in the head, or movement of the intestines, or some insignificant, usually unpleasant memory. A vast majority of the so-called "transcendental" experiences we ordinarily describe as psychosis. In fact, a number of cases of ecstatic experiences which were part of a full-blown psychosis are reported. In one case, a 38-year-old teacher of music who happened to be under great stress reported alteration of subjective awareness that made him view familiar things as if for the first time and investigate them with a "profound, exciting meaning." He found that he could understand nature, people, and animals better and had felt that "God actually touched his heart." However, the following day he experienced a mixture of "horror and ecstasy." Finally, he made a serious suicide attempt (Russel, 1959, p. 91).

Another psychosis-related case concerns a 21-year-old college student who was also under stress, which led to the following psychological developments during a week prior to his admission to a psychiatric institution (this case is fairly typical and will be quoted extensively):

> Before last week, I was quite closed about my emotions; then I finally owned up to them with another person. I began to speak without thinking beforehand and what came out showed an awareness of human beings and God. I could feel deeply about other people. We felt connected. The side which had been suppressing emotions did not seem to be the real one. I was in a higher and higher state of exhilaration and awareness. Things people said had hidden meaning. They said things that applied to life. Everything that was real seemed to make sense. I had a great awareness of life, truth and God. I went to Church, and suddenly all parts of the service made sense. My senses were sharpened. I became fascinated by the little insignificant things around me. There was an additional awareness of the

world that would do artists, architects, and painters good. I ended up being too emotional, but I felt very much at home with myself, very much at ease. It gave me a great feeling of power. It was not a case of seeing more broadly but deeper. I was losing touch with the outside world and lost my sense of time. There was a fog around me in some sense, and I felt half-asleep. I could see more deeply into problems that other people had and would go directly into a deeper subject with a person. I had the feeling I loved everybody in the world. Sharing emotions was like wiping the shadow away, wiping a false face. I thought I might wake up from a nightmare; ideas were pulsating through me. I became concerned that I might get violent so I called the doctor (Laing, 1967, p. 121).

He was admitted to a hospital in a severely agitated state expressing delusional ideas and ideas of reference (believing that whatever was happening around him was in some mysterious manner connected with his personal preoccupations). This case is typical in many respects. As in some mystical states, perception of "realness" was sharply increased. As pointed out earlier, there is evidence that in our old brain there is a system which, when stimulated directly, will provoke, completely out of context, a feeling that literally everything that impinges upon one's perception is endowed with an extraordinary sense of "realness." Aldous Huxley in *The Doors of Perception* expressed this sharpened sense of reality when he spoke of seeing: "Eternity in a flower, Infinity in four chair legs and the Absolute in the folds of a pair of flannel trousers" (Huxley, 2009).

Objectively speaking, there is no more validity in this distortion of perception than there is in seeing everything, say, "larger" or "more rounded." We often talk glibly about "tapping the hidden resources of the unconscious." We naively forget that in psychology, as well as in physics, ecology, and economics, there is an immutable law which states, "There is no such thing as a free lunch." In other words, you have to pay for everything, in one way or another. If you tap one resource to a greater than usual degree, something else may become "untapped." If you choose to consciously process one aspect of the world, another may slip into the realm of the unconscious. If you see everything greener than usual then you might not see yellow as sharply; if you see all colours more sharply, you may start missing on some sounds. If you hear sounds better and see colours better, it means that some higher integrating perceptual function is going to suffer, and so on. In this particular case, the sense of reality was increased out of all proportion, and yet the person recognized that he was losing his touch with the outside world and becoming disoriented in time. His senses were supposedly sharpened, and yet he felt that there was "a fog around him" and that he was "half asleep." He felt that he loved everybody and yet was afraid, probably with good reason, that he might become violent.

In some circles, there is a tendency to regard these psychotic experiences as "super-sane," as something we should almost strive for. In the popular mind, this trend in psychological thought is usually associated with the name of R. D. Laing (1967). One of the latest examples is a more moderate but still emphatic attempt to highlight the creative and renewing aspects of psychosis, undertaken by John Weir Perry (1989, 1999). While it is true that our superior-minded attitude towards mental patients is totally unwarranted and that our treatment of them is often callous and damaging, I also believe that anyone's misconceptions about the "super-sanity" of the mentally ill will be quickly cured by extensive encounters with people who suffer from psychosis, even if this happens outside the supposedly harmful confines of the mental institution. Their distress is often evident and real, as is their incapacity to manage even simple interpersonal relationships (Lazarus et al., 1965, pp. 622-635). The only "super-sane" people in mental institutions are the malingerers, who would immediately discard their view of reality when threatened with a potentially hazardous treatment such as electrical shock. A schizophrenic will, on the contrary, be unable to manage his environment successfully and will suffer as a result (Breakey, 1974, pp. 255-261).

Heightened cross-talk and rechannelling of awareness into unaccustomed paths can also be brought about by chemical means. One example of this, an injection of Metrazol, has already been given. Other better-known examples concern the use of such psychotropic[f] substances as LSD, psilocybin, mescalin, DMT, STP, and a host of other agents which are supposed to induce chemical ecstasy. It is a fact that their ingestion can produce experiences indistinguishable from those reported by traditional mystics The connection between, on the one hand, psychosis and the aberrations of metabolism of certain cerebral amines (such as catechol and serotonin) and, on the other, the capacity of

---

[f] There is a confusing variety of terms describing drugs, which affect human consciousness: "psychedelic" — mind-opening; "psycholythic" — mind-releasing; "hallucinogenic" — hallucination-provoking; "psychotomimetic" — psychosis-imitating; "psychotropic" — conscious-altering. The last one appears to be the most neutral and will be adhered to.

such drugs as LSD to interfere with these metabolic processes in the brain is now well known, even though the exact mechanics of this interaction are still far from clear. The effect of substances such as LSD on the metabolism of the cerebral amines in relation to the limbic system has also been experimentally shown (Bowers & Friedman, 1966, pp. 240 -248).

One investigator described the effects of LSD on the human brain in this fashion:

> From the existing evidence, it appears that the entire brain is not involved. It is in the diencephalon, or midbrain that the extraordinary events occur. This region contains the limbic system, which modulates emotional responsivity; the reticular formation, which regulates awareness; and the sympathetic and parasympathetic centres, which control dozens of physiologic functions, from pupil size to body temperature.

It seems certain that such psychotropic substances as LSD loosen physiological barriers in the brain and allow the individual to gain a perception of psychological functions which are ordinarily either inaccessible to the conscious perception or are available in integrated and highly "diluted" form. Those who have taken such drugs will testify as to the difference between a sense of unity in ordinary awareness ("we are from the same town") and the powerful state of unity ("I am all, and all is me") which is experienced in drug-induced states.

At the same time, it would be impossible to deny that many experiences of a mystical nature, whether in psychosis or drug experiences, are viewed, at least subjectively, as beneficial. R. D. Laing's Jesse, even though he ended by being locked up in a mental institution where with a bit of bad luck he could have remained for the rest of his life, still thought that this event heralded a meaningful change in his psychic life. The music teacher, whose case was quoted earlier and who nearly ended his life in a suicide, still regarded his experience as being profoundly meaningful and memorable. It appears that *subjectively* almost anything we do to alter our ordinary state of awareness, no matter how objectively damaging, may be regarded as a breakthrough. This is primarily an indication that something must be drastically wrong with our ordinary states of consciousness. The widespread use of psychotropic substances and even crude habit-forming and consciousness-modifying substances such as tobacco and alcohol attests that this is the case. The use of consciousness-altering drugs and plants, when used correctly, may help us to "reset" our brain to a more "holistic," "primitive," and less confused, traumatized and disjointed state.

The effect of psychotropic drugs on creativity was investigated on a number of occasions. In one study, four prominent artists were given LSD before a painting session. A panel of art critics reviewed their efforts. As it turned out, the paintings were bolder and more colorful, but the technical execution was somewhat inferior. However, the paintings were judged to be of better aesthetic value than the artists' usual work. Subjectively, the experience was also judged to be of positive value. As one artist expressed it, "I looked out of the window into the infinitely splendid universe of a tiny mauve leaf performing a cosmic ballet." In another study, psilocybin was administered to a number of creative individuals. Even though subjectively the experience proved to be extremely rewarding, it was found that as the effects of the drug began to wear off, the work that they were so impressed with a few minutes ago was losing its attractiveness (Cohen, 1967, p. 36). As one artist summed it up: "I have seldom known such absolute identification with what I was doing – nor such a lack of concern with it afterwards."

Application of psychotropic drugs was also tried in the case of a creative deadlock. A number of professional people who unsuccessfully worked for weeks or months on a particular problem were instructed to find a solution while under the influence of mescalin. Nearly all subjects came up with a solution which was subjectively judged highly creative and practicable. About half of these solutions led to a practical outcome (such as acceptance of a design by a client), while another half opened up new avenues of investigation. Again, three factors should not be forgotten: a) the individuals concerned did a lot of preliminary research on their projects; b) they were highly skilled and were in the fields of research which are, on the whole, permissive towards unusual solutions; c) the subjects were put into a stimulating situation which alone could have accounted for at least some of the breakthroughs. (There was no control group.) However, there can be no doubt that some significant alterations of ordinary creative processes were observed and that reports of enhanced creativity continued even after the drug wore off.

Chapter 1. The "Sacred Disease" and Other Paranormal States | 67

Dr Andrew Weil, "guru" of the alternative
holistic medical health with Pyotr Patrushev in Arizona (1977).

At one point, optimistic reports like the one above led some people to believe that they could open up some dormant resources of creativity by just taking psychotropic drugs. One study performed on an unselected group of people tested not only creativity but also performance in various psychological tests. The group consisted of volunteer graduate students who were not especially prominent in any particular field. The only test in which the LSD group did significantly better, compared with the control group, was one for the originality of word association. Tests that required visual attention and concentration were, on the contrary, performed very poorly by the LSD group. The authors of the study had to conclude that "the administration of LSD-25 to a relatively unselected group of people for the purpose of enhancing their creative ability is not likely to be successful." This conclusion is borne out by practical observations. After many decades of mass experimentation with consciousness-altering substances, we are still waiting for a cornucopia of freshly baked Huxleys, Baudelairs, and Dostoyevskys that, as it was widely hoped, it would produce. Apparently, one has to be more or less a genius before one can greatly benefit from a transcendental experience, however, induced.

Thus, it would appear that the vast majority of cases of the so-called "expanded awareness" into the subcortical areas through recreational drug use without supervision and training, and with random quality substances, are, like most spontaneous genetic mutations, detrimental to the well-being, health or success of the individual. Because most of us are not aware of the underlying universal mechanisms of "transcendence," we tend to single out only the relatively beneficial experiences and forget the detrimental ones. I suppose that people who have undergone the negative type of transcendental experience are much less likely to write reports about it. However, even in the description of the "good" experiences there is a fair admixture of "bad" components. The symptoms of saintliness described earlier in the discussion of epilepsy can hardly be considered desirable by most people and have even given rise to the notion of the "saint's malaise." A careful reading of many autobiographical accounts of the so-called transcendental experiences will convince most people that they are dealing with something that is far from a straightforward blissful affair. They are, at best, a mixed bag. There are numerous sites that contain current and detailed descriptions of experiences with psychedelics, notably Erowid.org and Reset.me

Most cases of spontaneously provoked transcendence – in epilepsy, psychosis, accidental "ecstasies," drug-induced experiences – are a stab in the dark. Only very seldom, and in most cases by sheer chance, do we hit the jackpot by achieving regular or lasting ecstasy. A testament to this claim is the fact that there are far more psychotics who have known the terrible agony of reality slipping away from under their feet than there are mystics who have known the "supreme joy" of reality lost and found. This is hardly surprising. The limbic system and the human brain as a whole is a highly complex and unstable structure. The emphasis on "expansion of awareness at all costs" appears ill-founded. If we become, for example, conscious of the hypothalamic functions which regulate water or heat balance, we would probably create complete chaos in our lives. Even the largest computer would be unable to perform all the actions, in the right sequence, necessary to digest a potato. However, if we leave things to themselves, these tremendous feats of efficiency are usually accomplished quite easily.

At the same time, it is hard to draw a line between the "natural" and "unnatural" consciousness-modifying methods. The traditional mystic or a yogi who is indulging in forced breathing, fasting, flagellation, sensory deprivation and so forth, is judged by some to act strictly in accordance with the natural order of things. The drug user who produces similar states through more direct interference with the brain biochemistry is seen as violating this supposedly preordained order. Entire books have been written to prove the difference between the two types of experience. Of course, differences can be found. Upon careful analysis, no two "natural" transcendental experiences are identical. If anything, the side effects of a drug-induced religious experience, if done under the careful guidance and in congenial settings, are probably less damaging to the mind and the body than the masochistic, paraphernalia-ridden, mystical pursuits of the past. One may also successfully argue for the use of psychotropic drugs in far-gone and therapy-resistant cases of psychosis and terminal physical illness. There is now a renewed interest in the research into psychedelic plants and their therapeutic and other uses (MAPS, 2016). The American Psychological Association has noted "the benefits of these illegal drugs may outweigh the risks in certain scenarios," and "the drugs may help improve functioning and lift the spirits of those with cancer and other terminal diseases, as well as help treat people with post-traumatic stress disorder" (Medical Daily, 2016).

In my book *Project Nirvana: How the War on Drugs was Won* (Patrushev, 2014), I explore, albeit fictionally, the possibility of using psychotropic substances for general health promotion and suggest how psychedelically catalyzed meditation (PCM) can be used to combat drug and alcohol addiction, improve productivity and general well-being.[g]

Such experiments must be done under rigorous controls, using only the safest psychedelics, preferably in micro doses that are carefully titrated and gradually reduced to a zero, and in conjunction with well-tested meditation techniques such as mindfulness meditation as the main vehicle of consciousness stabilization and expansion ("Mindfulness," n.d.). Careful and constant monitoring of progress is accomplished by a combination of simple, inexpensive, and well-tested somatic and psychological tests, such as heart

---

[g] http://goo.gl/tr7vjH

rate variability (HRV) and hypnotic induction profile (HIP[h]) and a whimsical, practical example that proved to be very popular with student viewers.[i]

---
[h] http://goo.gl/tr7vjH
[i] http://goo.gl/KZuQ15

Chapter 2.
The Sanskrit Cookbook

I. To Seize the Moment...

"Der den Augenblick ergereift Das ist der rechte Mann."
"He who seizes the moment is the right man."
Goethe

There is one more reason to think that the ecstatic experience is, if not abnormal, then very unusual: it is nearly always brief. The nervous system is unable to maintain significant levels of cross talk along unaccustomed channels for great lengths of time. It is as if a spark would now and again jump from one end of an insulated pole to another. However, the steady current is not allowed to build up. This is true of both the spontaneous transcendence and the drug-induced ecstasy. What inevitably follows is the "coming down." This mainly concerns experiences that are profoundly blissful.

There seems to be a contradiction. On the one hand, the experience is extremely attractive on the other; it is *so* attractive that the person cannot tolerate it. Dostoyevsky says that if the ecstatic aura lasted "more than five seconds –

the soul would not be able to endure it and would have to dissolve... to endure ten seconds *one would have to change physically"* (emphasis added). St Augustine (2012) also speaks of this in his Confessions:

> Thus with the flash of one trembling glance it [the soul] arrived at That Which Is. And then I saw Thy invisible things understood by the things, which are made. But I could not fix my gaze thereupon; and my infirmity being struck back, I was thrown again on my wonted habits, carrying along with me only a loving memory thereof, and a longing for what I had, as it were, perceived the odour of, but was not yet able to feel on.

Jesse, the hero of R. D. Laing's *Ten-day Voyage* (Laing, 1967) also gives expression to his inability to maintain the state of awareness, which he reached halfway through his psychic journey:

> I didn't have the capacity for experiencing it. I experienced it for a moment or two, but it was a sudden blast of light, wind, or whatever you like to put it as against you so that you feel you're too naked and alone to be able to withstand it, you're not strong enough.

In the human brain, various functions are often lumped together and housed, so to speak, in the same compartment. The genital area is closely related to that which regulates food intake and perception of smell, while emotions that accompany rage excite such bodily changes as the acceleration of heartbeat, dilation of bronchi, and inhibition of the bladder wall. The extent of these physical changes depends upon the degree of the emotion felt. It would follow that experience of an incredibly powerful ("pure") sensation of some kind would trigger physical changes that are beyond the usual physiological limits, and which the body would therefore be unable to maintain. In fact, one cannot speak about the various changes mentioned as triggering one another – physiologically they all come in one amorphous lump. Thus, a profound experience of bliss and the suspension of breath, the slowing down of heart rate, the inhibition of salivary flow, the tendency to burp, and the constriction of pupils may all happen simultaneously.

I remember my initial puzzlement of J. P. Sartre's choice of a title *Nausea* for a book (Sartre & Alexander, 2007) that, describes a case of a spontaneous transcendence accompanied by an incredibly vivid perception of "realness." This sensation appears to belong to the same breathless and restful category as the feeling of bliss. The bodily changes that presumably accompany it indicate that it is the parasympathetic division of the autonomic nervous system, which is active at the time of such experiences. Physiologists know that *overstimulation* of the parasympathetic centres can result in nausea. I have also encountered unrecorded reports of slight nauseousness experienced by meditators during some meditations. A similar phenomenon is an emission of air (like a small burp), which is also a result of parasympathetic overstimulation. The increased gastric motility will tend to push trapped air from the upper alimentary tract and bring it up as a burp. See my humorous <u>Burping and Enlightenment</u> (Patrushev, 2014a).

76 | The Transcendent Ape

A feeling of bliss. (Fiantsev, 2017c)

It is very difficult to predict the exact nature of the physiological changes which may accompany some particularly powerful "transcendent" sensations triggered off somewhere in the limbic system. (It makes one wonder if St. Augustine was only using metaphors when he spoke of "the odour" which he perceived but was unable to "feed on.") One thing is certain: the body will find it difficult to endure these peculiar changes for a prolonged period. And so the mind will only retain "a loving memory" of the state it was in. Only in psychosis will the limbic disorganization have a "scattered" enough character, with possible counterbalancing tendencies, to make it possible to maintain various subjective states of reality distortion.

Similar considerations apply to the use of psychotropic drugs. Their effect on the limbic system is of a relatively "blanket" order, thus entailing counterbalancing physiological effects. It is known that LSD-25 produces powerful changes not only on the cerebral but also on the autonomic level. It brings about an increased sensitivity to stimuli in all modalities. The non-selective nature of the psychotropic drugs implies that they may activate not only the "Heaven" but also the "Hell" systems in the brain. The person who is having a "bad trip" may experience sensations of utter blackness, fear and isolation (Rachman, 1974, pp. 18-19). The brilliant colours that one sees on a "good trip" turn into strange greens and frightening dark reds. The face seen in the mirror may all of a sudden begin to shrink and decay; everything around may appear unreal, dead, puppet-like.

The dependence of mystical states upon certain physical triggers has long been recognized by mystical and religious aspirants. We know that under all types of religious cloaks the sensitive noses of the eager believers were, throughout the ages, subjected to olfactory bombardment (burning incense, camphor, etc.). The communion with all sorts of deities seemed to be uniformly enhanced by this apparently irrelevant ritualistic activity. There is no better way to activate the deep limbic circuitry than to stimulate the olfactory sense, which is closely connected to some of the oldest structures in the brain, including the pleasure circuitry.

Various types of rhythmic auditory stimulation, from tom-toms to hymn singing, also represent an almost universal feature of religious ritual. All these "facilitation techniques" are capable of producing profound religious experiences only in people with high cross-talk potential. The most an ordinary believer, who is not blessed with a peculiar brain (dis) organization, would get out of his religious pursuits would be a slight sense of euphoria due to an emotionally charged atmosphere of a church gathering, with all its attendant incense-burning and hymn chanting. Certainly, the epileptic Prince Myshkin, or a lucky mescalin user, or even a psychotic patient with electrodes implanted in his brain would know much more of the proverbial "Kingdom of Heaven" than countless numbers of lay and professional religious believers. In Laski's analysis of transcendental ecstatic experiences quoted above, there are virtually no experiences which have been induced by regular religious practices (such as communal or individual prayer).

Even religious mystics tended to recognize that the triggering circumstances of their most intensive ecstatic states were outside of purposeful religious effort. In her *Way of Perfection* St. Teresa Avila (2013) states, "This is a supernatural thing which we cannot obtain by any effort on our part." On the other hand, supposedly religious triggers may work just as well with complete non-believers who may happen to have a high T.Q. In one case, quoted by Laski, an ecstatic experience was triggered in an atheist by, of all things, reading of the *Bible*. It may be significant that he describes his experience as "a mixture of physical attack and cerebral confusion – sadness mixed with joy." I am not suggesting that he may have been a victim of the so-called "reading epilepsy" (a rare type of epilepsy triggered by reading) but that in his case the subject matter of his reading may not have been as important as some other circumstances. His other triggers were, by the way, singing, music, and poetry.

The fact that faith alone, as well as indulgence in rituals, has only rarely and accidentally brought about profound mystical experiences was well recognized. Both in the Occident and, more specifically, in the Orient, techniques have been devised that were supposed to facilitate the more direct transition into the higher states of consciousness. In the Orient, these methods became recognized, with the result that some peculiar breathing technique in conjunction with abdominal contractions came to be viewed as quite a legitimate means of contacting the "higher reality." Recognizing this paradox, the more honest exponents of Oriental religions accepted the experience on its own merits and refused to attach any supernatural significance to it. *The Upanishads* (Eknath & Nagler, 2007), a collection of Indian sacred scriptures, state quite specifically that it is possible to obtain "a uniformed state with the Brahman [the Supreme Being] using restraint of breath, withdrawal of senses, meditation, concentration, contemplation and absorption".

In the Christian West, however, the purposeful techniques practised by monks and mystics were looked upon with some uneasiness. Thus in the forward to the *Writings from the Philokalia* (a collection of writings by the Fathers of the Eastern Church from the 4th-14th centuries) it is written that the "Practice of the Jesus Prayer is the traditional fulfilment of the injunction of the Apostle Paul to 'pray always;' it has nothing to do with the mysticism which is the heritage of pagan ancestry" (Palmer & Kadloubovsky, 1977, p. 5). What is the Jesus Prayer and how different is it from other "mystical and pagan" techniques? The instructions for meditation on the Jesus Prayer are given as follows:

> So, sitting down in your cell, collect your mind, lead it into the path of the breath along which the air enters in, constrain it to enter the heart together with the inhaled air, and keep it there. Keep it there, but do not leave it silent and idle; instead give it the following prayer: 'Lord Jesus Christ, Son of God, have mercy upon me' (Kotsonis, 1997).

This method, if practised diligently and continuously will lead to a state of union with the soul, which is "filled with unspeakable sweetness and joy" (ibid).

Here we have all the essential elements which characterize most Oriental meditation techniques, namely, sensory deprivation, concentration, rhythmic application of a "mantra" (a sacred phrase, word, or syllable), which may or may not be attached to a particular part of the body or a bodily activity, and a resulting state of perfect bliss (Nirvana, Satori, etc.). It may be argued that whereas in, for example, a corresponding Zen meditation the concentration is on the breath and the meaningless counting of the breaths, here we have a meaningful invocation whose effect is presumed to be quite different. We learn, however, that even the Jesus Prayer, with practice, undergoes certain changes, which tend to strip it of its intellectual and devotional overtones:

> After many years of struggle, the advanced sweep away all imagination, both proper and improper, so that no trace of it remains. As wax melts in the fire, so does imagination disperse and disappear under the action of pure prayer... (ibid, pp. 192-3).

The goal of this type of meditation is to "take the prayer down into the 'heart' where it lives itself with every heartbeat" (ibid, p. 235). It would seem that the practitioners of this meditation could have saved themselves many years of struggle if they had shortened their invocation to manageable proportions, compatible with their breath or the rate of the heartbeat. We can see that the practitioner is wasting the first few months or even years of his practice simply to "decorticalize" the prayer until it becomes a meaningless vibration, which can be harmonized with breath and heartbeat. In fact, the Fathers themselves made certain concessions to practical demands by allowing, for example, to split the prayer into two and to use both halves alternatively. They could not, however, go as far as the anonymous author of the medieval mystical treatise, *The Cloud of the Unknowing* (Gallacher, 1997), who also recommends concentration on the heart, but in conjunction with a much shorter mantra:

And if the list has this intent lapped and folded in one word, *for thou shoulders have better hold thereupon*, take thee but a little word of one syllable; for so it is better than of two, forever the shorter it is, the better it affordeth with the work of the spirit. And such a word is this word GOD or this LOVE. Choose thee whether thou wilt, or another; as thee list, which that thee liketh best of one syllable. And fasten this word to thine heart so that it never go thence for thing that befalleth...

We remember that the frequencies that produce spillover effects in the brain are relatively fast. Naturally, the effective frequencies produced by the mental repetition of the prayer of the heart should be in the range of 70-80 per minute (frequency of heartbeat). The mantra should be sufficiently short to generate such a frequency. In general, it seems that the more esoteric the tradition, the shorter the mantra. At the other extreme, there are the long Christian mantras. It is possible, however, that people with long experience in meditation (or people who have a naturally high T.Q. which would probably include most prominent mystics and yogis) can use longer mantras effectively. Analysing various meditation techniques, we almost invariably find that some rhythmic repetitive activity, or at least an awareness of some rhythmic repetitive activity, is involved. In various yogic techniques, it is the repetition of a mantra, with or without concentration on breathing or certain parts of the body (chakras). In Buddhism, the so-called "mindfulness of breathing" (Anapanasati) falls into the same category. The meditator is instructed to keep his attention on the breath, either counting the successive breaths or just passively following the passage of the air. Alternatively, as a stage in the above meditation, or as a separate meditation technique (the Burmese *Satipatthana*), the meditator watches the regular rising and falling movement of the abdomen, resulting from breathing.

In Sufism (an Islamic mystical tradition) there is a meditation practice known as "Dhikr," which also involves repetition of a sacred sound (a "wird") in conjunction with rhythmic dancing, music, and recitation of musical poetry. In Shintoism (native to Japan), some practices involve rhythmic breathing, counting or repetition of sacred words, combined with a steady gaze at the mirror. Various Shamanistic rites practised by the peoples of North and South America, Indonesia, Oceania, Africa, Siberia, and Japan involve songs or chants which are performed to a musical accompaniment (usually that of a drum) and are designed to bring on an ecstatic trance.

II. The Way of the Simple Regard

Aside from their basic similarity, the various approaches to meditation can be separated into two distinct categories: those, which demand effort and concentration and those which imply passivity of attitude, a kind of "watchful awareness."

The Philokalia does not give one universal rule (Palmer & Kadloubovsky, 1977). On the one hand, some Fathers, not unexpectedly, announce "the fruit of inner prayer of the heart requires long work and forcing oneself, and in general, everything good is attained by long and strenuous effort." Only to some, they admit, God, in His inscrutable ways, accords "this achievement" by "simple happening." These lucky ones are said to "quake, being filled with joy," undergoing what the Fathers called the "leaping of joy" (Eph. 3:17).

With what has been said earlier about the length of the mantra used and all the conscious associations it must have carried, it is perhaps no wonder that the vast majority of monks found the Prayer of Jesus "long work and strenuous effort." Judging by the questions which they asked of the enlightened Fathers, most of them never went beyond the futile struggle with their imagination, sexual fantasies, etc., and never partook of the "unspeakable bliss" that the selected ones were enjoying. Most of the book actually deals not so much with any advanced experiences by the seekers, but with their routine and mundane conditioning into certain ways of behaviour: what to do if one has a nocturnal emission, what sort of food to eat, whether to look or not look at women, or what to do if a fight between brothers breaks out.

In accordance with *The Philokalia*, during the meditation itself, one is advised to "firmly sweep away...wrong imagination...the abode of barren and passionate thoughts."

On the other hand, the advanced practitioners "after many years of struggle...sweep away all imagination, both proper and improper." So, there is perhaps not so much difference in approach as a difference in the degree of absorption in meditation, which at first requires unfailing concentration but later becomes effortless. The emphasis on effort entirely lacks in many Oriental traditions. In the *Buddhist Lankavatara* Sutra it is explicitly stated that any attempt to drive away imagination and thoughts will be counter-productive:

Disciples sometimes think that they can expedite the attainment of their goal of tranquillisation by entirely suppressing the activities of the mind system. This is a mistake, for even if the activities of the mind are suppressed, the mind will still go on functioning because the seeds of habit-energy will remain (Humphreys, 1998, p. 169).

This advice reminds one of the famous "law of the reversed effort" first stated by C. Baudouin:

> The law of reversed effort is revealed in all simplicity to anyone who is learning to ride a bicycle. When we are at length able to wobble painfully along, should we see a big stone lying in the middle of the road, we know that all our attempts to avoid it serve only to direct our steering wheel towards the obstacle, upon which it impinges with deadly precision. The stone has attracted our attention, the suggestion is at work, and our efforts to counteract it serve merely to reinforce it (Baudouin, & Paul, 2016, p. 116).

In contrast with this, St. Teresa sees the necessity for effort at least during the "lower" degrees of prayer. Thus she compares the first degree with drawing water from a deep well by hand; the second degree to the use of a windlass in drawing water; the third degree to a river which irrigates the garden by itself; and the fourth degree to completely effortless watering of the garden by God's rain.

In general, we find that the activities of the intellect are looked upon by most mystics as a barrier on the path of meditation. This anti-intellectual tendency reaches its height in the writings of Nicholas of Cusa (2005), a 15th century mystic and philosopher. He says: "Thou, God, who art infinity, canst only be approached by him whose intellect is in ignorance, to wit, by him who knows himself to be ignorant of Thee" (Happold, 1970, pp. 343-54).

One must enter into darkness, beyond all the grasp of reason, before the seemingly irreconcilable opposites coincide.

This idea is also akin to the Zen Buddhist thought which implies a rejection of intellectual understanding in favour of direct experiencing. The Zen Buddhists use a technique of "koan" to achieve the necessary transference from intellectual to intuitive levels of cognition. A koan is a phrase, a puzzle, which appears meaningless to the rational mind. Typical koans are: "Two hands when clapped make a certain sound. What is the sound of one hand clapping?" "What was your original face before your parents were born?" The Zen meditator struggles unsuccessfully with one of these conundrums. Through an ever-increasing pressure of "searching and contriving" the mind is gradually led to "a state of intellectual bankruptcy." With his mind in a thorough state of exhaustion, the student "leaps over the precipice" and finds "enlightenment." Here we see how the "law of reversed effort" is made to operate against itself: the mind is stilled through purposeful overuse (everything in Zen is paradoxical – we avoid the stone on the road by driving directly at it, millions of times, until utterly exhausted.)

We can now summarize some of the universal principles, which underlie the meditative practices discussed above:

In most of them, we have some repetitive stimulus, which, through an active process of concentration or a passive one of "the simple regard," leads the meditator's attention into the deep non-intellectual areas of the mind, which also contain sensations of "pure bliss." Any intellectual activity will be detrimental to the process, unless it is consciously aimed to tire the intellect so that, in the words of a leading Zen exponent Dr. Suzuki, "it's more central and profounder parts which are generally deeply buried can be brought out and exercised to perform their native functions" (ibid. 343-54).

We can also tie this up with the details of neurophysiology discussed in previous chapters. The areas of "bliss" are found in the old part of the human brain, the limbic system. This part of the brain operates on a non-logical, non-verbal level. To activate it, the thinking capacity of the neocortex must be minimized. This is accomplished by either meditation on a meaningless mantra, or by the process of cortical inhibition through tiring, which will bring on a compensatory excitation of the subcortical areas. The inhibited cortex enters into a "paradoxical state," when a well-timed minute stimulus – the "koan," the movement of a teacher's finger, the flower he shows to a pupil – can tip the balance and bring about a total reversal of previous conditioning. The mind gains access to the subconscious areas, which house "pure understanding" and becomes "enlightened."

This is all well and good, but what are the neural dynamics of the opposite approach, that of passive attentiveness to the operation of one's mantra? We remember that in flicker stimulation tests, only a small proportion of subjects (3-4%) responded to a fixed flicker frequency. This frequency had to be constantly adjusted to be kept in harmony with the spontaneous rhythm of the brain. When this is accomplished by a feedback arrangement that automatically fires the flicker in synchrony with any brain wave pattern chosen, the crosstalk effects are produced much more easily (in 50% of all cases).

In meditation, we have a comparable picture. If there is any concentration entailing the use of willpower, this may tend to keep the frequency of the excitation independent of the spontaneous rhythmic activity of the deep areas of the brain. In other words, it will correspond to the "no feedback" variety of the flicker test: the conscious brain keeps firing the mantra, or whatever, at its pace. Perhaps once in a while, the lucky combination will be hit upon and the spill over effect will occur. However, the conscious mind will probably terminate this effect by going back to the consciously pre-determined frequency ("I must keep saying that Jesus Prayer in full").

The professed goal of most types of meditation discussed above is to bring about the "beatific vision," the "supreme bliss," etc. It is natural to assume that at some stage in meditation the activation of the pleasure circuitry will produce the point of attraction, towards which the attention of the meditator will become spontaneously directed. Cybernetically, we have all the elements essential for an internal self-steering feedback mechanism. We have the repetitive stimulus (the mantra), the spontaneous rhythms in the brain, and the third factor – attractiveness of the bliss areas that will exercise a directing influence on the previous two to achieve the rewarding cross-talk effect. In other words, the mantra, if left to itself, will tend to find the effective frequency, which will produce the desired goal – the perception of bliss. The more experienced meditators apparently spontaneously realize this. For example, St. Nilus, quoted in *The Philokalia*, says, "attention seeking prayer will find prayer" (Nilus, 1975).

Does this mean that if one chooses a mantra of some manageable length and one which preferably has no conscious associations, one's attention, if left to follow its natural course, will immediately go to the pleasure centres? This does not seem to be the case except, perhaps, with people who have an extremely high T.Q. First, the circuitry in the brain that is necessary to link the pleasure centres with our conscious awareness must be *directly* activated. Even though this circuitry may be presumed to be similar to the one which is involved in, say, procurement of pleasure through sex, there still must be considerable differences. Therefore, to excite the slightly different pathways, we must rely on the "breakdown" effect of rhythmic stimulation. There is a paradox! ***The mantra will lead attention to the area of bliss only when and if it becomes associated with bliss.***

We also know that the "pleasure" and "pain" circuits are mutually inhibiting. For one to become active, especially to the degree associated with a perception of intensive "pure" pleasure, the other one has to be inhibited or inactive. Besides, the direct activation of the pleasure circuit automatically means activation of the relaxation circuit. The body must be capable of attaining an unnaturally deep degree of relaxation for the mind to be able to perceive an unnaturally intense degree of pleasure and maintain it for a considerable period.

In ordinary physiological states, pleasure can be associated with both sympathetic and parasympathetic activity. Thus, laughter is a sympathetic response and is obviously pleasant. In contrast, weeping is a parasympathetic response and is generally, though not always, unpleasant. Mixed or mutually reinforcing reactions can also occur (Valentstein, & Beer, 1964, pp. 183–184). Listening attentively to a beautiful piece of music (parasympathetic) may produce a high state of arousal (sympathetic). The most paradoxical state is found in sex. The erection is, apparently, a parasympathetic and ejaculation a sympathetic response. Yet orgasm quite obviously is one of the most pleasant states experienced by humans. As has been mentioned earlier, the aggressive nature of sexual drive can explain its sympathetic quality.

In a sense, Nature had to strike a sort of neurological compromise to preserve the aggressive nature of sex while at the same time making it attractive (pleasant). The compromise is reflected in three aspects of orgasmic pleasure: it is very brief; it is accompanied by almost epilepsy-like convulsions indicating a peculiar nature of the neurological discharge; and it is followed by a rebound state of deep relaxation which is nearly as pleasant as the orgasm itself[j]

---

[j] The research on endorphins indicates that these substances produce a cooling and tranquillising effect on the nervous system (as do all opiates). These recent discoveries support this author's thesis that the "pleasure response" experienced by the mystic and the Tantric practitioner is parasympathetic in nature.

III. To Scour the Windows of the Soul

All these neurological factors have long been recognized by the traditional mystics who placed much emphasis on the preliminary "purification" necessary for the attainment of the ultimate goal. Transcendence by an unprepared mind is fraught with dire consequences, they warned. At the beginning of the practice, states *The Philokalia:*

> There comes the spirit of fear, rending the mountains of passions and breaking in pieces the rocks – hardened hearts – such fear that the flesh seems to be pierced by nails and numbed as in death (Eph. 3:17).

The need for the "continuous cleansing of the perception and a scouring of the windows of the soul" is continually emphasized in the mystical literature. In his *The Ascent of Mount Caramel* St. John of the Cross (2015) speaks of the necessity of passing through two dark nights of the soul until one attains the state of perfection. St. Teresa of Avila (2005) speaks, in *The Interior Castle,* of the "Seven Mansions" which correspond to stages of progress in spiritual life. The courtyard of the castle is cold, dark, and filled with all sorts of obnoxious and poisonous creatures. It is only the inner part that is full of light.

The science of purification has reached its highest development in various techniques of yoga. A yogic scripture, *Gheranda Samhita* (Kulvalayananda, 2014), lists the following means of purification (*shodana*):

- By means of posture (*asana*), strength (*dridhata*) comes about;
- By means of exercise (*mudra*), steadiness (*sthirata*);
- By means of withholding the senses (*pratyahara*), bodily calmness (*dhirata*) ;
- By ordering the breath (*pranayama*), lightness (*laghava*);
- By meditation (*dhyana*), vision of oneself (*pratyaksham atmanah*);
- By contemplation (*samadhi*), unstainedness (*nirlipta*),
- In addition, even freedom (*mukti*); etc.

One must not, however, form an impression that there is a complete uniformity amongst the various mystical traditions in relation to these preliminary procedures of self-purification. The emphasis can be vastly different, as, for example, in Christian mysticism and yoga. In the former, it is mostly the various techniques and suggestions for "mortifying" the body and the senses, which are emphasized, while in the latter, the body is brought to a state of physical perfection so that it becomes a suitable vehicle for the soul (Organ, 1970, p. 303). Moreover, different authors in different traditions put their individual emphasis on the aspects of purification, which they regard as quite essential. This creates a rather confusing picture in which the same goal may be attained by two diametrically opposed means.

Most spiritual leaders who have compiled these exertions probably had extremely high cross-talk potentials. We know from the cases described above that for them a mere looking into the blinking fire, reclining on a bed of nails, or a chance exposure to rhythmic chanting will do the trick.

"**Look into the fire**". (Fiantsev, 2017d)

To a person who links his experience with the circumstances that preceded or surrounded it, there is a causal link between the two. So he will tend to maintain that "this" (whether it is chanting, breathing exercises, or an ardent faith in the Lord) has paved the way for the transcendence.

In time, these teachings become stylized within their societies and are avidly followed by people who have the proof of their efficacy in the person of their leader, but who cannot get anywhere near the ideal themselves and tend to become bogged down in the mere ritual.

It is here where we can see how, in cultures throughout the world and throughout history where enlightenment through meditation is a gift striven for by many, those individuals who possessed especially high cross-talk potential or were predisposed to epilepsy might be

labelled as "blessed" rather than "cursed." For them, a neurological predisposition was something that elevated rather than condemned; it allowed them to see or achieve things that most of their society sought unsuccessfully. In this sense, they were extraordinary, not abnormal. Compare this situation with medieval Europe, where people with epilepsy were seen not to be inhabited by the Holy Spirit, but rather by demons. In most cases, these individuals were persecuted and killed, not offered religious tutelage. Thus, two rifts open up, each representing the separation between society and the spiritual leader/epileptic: the masses view one rift as the holy canyon that separates them from enlightenment or the Lord, the other is seen as the black gulf that separates them from the possessed.

A tremendous dichotomy is created between the leader and the led, the specially gifted ones, and the "normal" majority. The leader, who speaks from a different level of consciousness, is forced to communicate in similes and parables to convey the meaning of his revealing insights. The followers cannot, because of the rift that separates them neurologically from the leader, understand the true essence of these insights and simply incorporate them into their belief systems, thereby distorting them out of all recognition. When they try to obtain the direct experience themselves, they find that instead of unspeakable joy their minds are full of petty little thoughts and insignificant memories. Getting no immediate reward from their practice, they turn it into a mere ritual.

The experiences of an average meditator who is not blessed with the peculiar neurophysiology necessary for spontaneous transcendence are aptly described in the following account:

What I think when I meditate
Well, I could tell you that I could tell you but wouldn't understand but I won't
You'd understand but I can't, I mean dig,
This here guitar is gone bust I hate to sit cross-legged
My knees hurt my nose runs and I have to go
To the crapper
Tootsweet and damn that timeclock keeper won't ding.
WHAT I think about when I meditate is emptiness.
I remember it well
The empty heads the firecracker phhht
But what I really think about is sex
Sort of patterns of sex
Like dancing hairs and goosebumps
No, honestly
What I think about is what am I thinking about?
And who am I?
And "MU?" and "the clouds
On the southern mt"
Well: what I really honestly think about, no fooling...(etc.)

Various approaches are suggested for dealing with this problem of intruding thoughts. The Christian mystical approach tends, overall, to be rather aggressive. John of the Ladder tells us in the *Philokalia* "to flog our foes with the name Jesus" (Climacus, 1978). Gallacher in *The Cloud of Unknowing* (1997) after recommending choosing a word God or Love for meditation, further advises us "with this word, thou shalt beat on this cloud and this darkness above thee. With this word, thou shalt smite down all manner of thought under a cloud of forgetting." The Oriental approach is, by comparison, rather lenient. A Chinese saying recommends: "Let thoughts arise within your mind without repressing them and without being carried away by them. Let not the passing thought be annihilated, and let not a passing thought rise up again."

From our daily experience, we know that an upsurge of thoughts may accompany periods of attentive passivity. As soon as our minds are relatively unoccupied, the memory content begins to rise to the conscious level. (A psychiatrist who puts his patient on a couch in an easy and relaxed posture and asks him to tell whatever comes to his mind is utilizing this phenomenon.) In the deep relaxation, which accompanies meditation, dozens of memory traces begin to float up to the conscious level, gradually taking on the form of thoughts. If we pay conscious attention to their content, resist them, or begin to analyze them, we will attach more memory tags to them and facilitate their future retrieval. The thoughts that float up are not disembodied images. They are connected to emotions which, when aroused by memory, provoke physical changes.

So, in meditation, there is a tug of war going on between the process of relaxation, which makes thoughts rise up from the unconscious and the bodily changes that are produced by them upon arising.

Many spiritual teachers emphasize that the process of emptying memory content must be gradual. If this happens suddenly, as it does with a "bad" drug trip or in a psychotic experience, the mind gets flooded with painful memories and is unable to deal with them. In an effortless meditation of the Oriental type, however, the following things appear to happen. The attention, carried by the self-adjusting rhythmic vibration of the mantra, works its way through to the pleasure centres, activates the restful parasympathetic nervous system, and causes thoughts to float up and fill the void created in the conscious mind by the absence of external stimuli. It is possible, indeed probable, that memories are "recorded" together with the mode of hypothalamic activity, which predominated when they were felt. Their release in meditation against the background of the restful parasympathetic state will exercise a neutralising effect and will prevent their future associations with the "fight or flight" behaviour.

Here, one is reminded of the "desensitization" techniques used in the treatment of obsessive fears (Mathews, 1971, pp. 73-83). A patient is instructed to relive in his imagination (or even in reality) a step-by-step approach to the dreaded object. At the same time, he is taught to relax. Gradual association of the fearful stimuli with the state of relaxation (instead of tension) tends to loosen the customary physiological reactions and finally eliminates them completely. This method is found to be surprisingly effective. It also works without taking into account the origin of a particular fear.

Researchers have found that obsessive fears that would have otherwise required years of psychoanalysis to subvert were effectively abolished after 3-4 sessions of desensitization. Take the spider phobia for example. By the psychoanalytic interpretation, the fear of spiders is because it represents the dangerous (orally devouring and anally castrating) mother. The patients who suffer from this fear are said to have severe problems of sexual identity with a possible tendency to bisexuality. It would seem that if this particular fear were removed – and it is supposed to be nothing but a camouflage of these deeper problems of sexual identity – the patient would soon find some other neurotic outlet for it or acquire a new phobia. Nothing of the kind happens. The phobias are removed by this non-analytical method once and for all.

The thoughts that float up in meditation represent the tips of the emotive memory conglomerates, which are built by the processes of memory filing. In meditation, these memory conglomerates are broken down into their small and logically unrelated bits. These bits are desensitized one by one, and the whole pattern of the "complex" need not be perceived. If it is observed and analysed, it will be connected to some other memory, which would then be filed instead of the old one. This is probably what is meant by the Chinese saying: "Let not a passing thought rise again."

Meditation of the gentle, non-judgemental and restful type can be viewed as a process of global desensitization of accumulated body/mind stress.

IV. The Yogi and the Wolf

What is the result of this process? Finally, as emotional memories become dislodged, the thinking process acquires a freewheeling quality. It has been unhinged from the automatic subconscious connection to the memories. Lankavatara Sutra describes the ordinary state of awareness which gives rise to the process of "discrimination" which subtly shapes our actions:

> It is because the ignorant cling to names, signs and ideas; as their minds move along these channels they feed on multiplicities of objects and fall into the notion of an ego-soul and what belongs to it; they make discriminations of good and bad among appearances and cling to the agreeable. As they, thus, cling there is a *reversion to*

ignorance, and karma, born of greed, anger and folly is accumulated. As the accumulation of karma goes on, they become imprisoned in a cocoon of *discrimination* and are thenceforth unable to free themselves from the round of birth and death. (Pine, 2013).

Compare this to a startlingly similar contemporary scientific exposition belonging to one of our leading investigators of emotion and motivation:

> We can like or dislike only something we know. We must see or hear or touch something, remember having done so or imagined it before we can decide that it is good or bad for us. The sensation must be completed by some form of appraisal [Buddhist "discrimination"] before it can lead to action...Appraisal seems to be a process of evaluating and comparing sense impressions and memories from many sense modalities, and thus take an appreciable time. But once a thing is evaluated, the experience of liking or disliking it follows immediately and automatically [Buddhist "reversion to ignorance"].

When the connection between the thought, memories, and the emotions they evoke is loosened, "the cocoon of discrimination" is cut. The actions no longer automatically spring from memories. They acquire a "here and now" quality which comes from acute observation of the situation as it is.

The yoga and mystical books are full of glowing descriptions of the enlightened ones who have achieved "the serene and placid surface of the unruffled mind." There is, however, a fundamental question, which those books fail to answer. Can we have an "unruffled mind" and yet prevent ourselves from burning our fingers on a candle over and over again? Can we eliminate the abuses of the cortical tag attachment without eliminating its uses?

As one reads the popular yoga publications about enlightened sages who walked straight into the bush fire and got burnt to death without as much as a whimper, one begins to suspect that we cannot. (On the other hand, as one observes the much more shrewd behaviour of some real-life yogis, one starts to regain faith in the enlightened person's reasonableness after all.) The real situation is somewhat more complicated. An enlightened yogi with his "unruffled mind" may be at a slight survival disadvantage in a physically precarious environment if he does not break into a headlong flight whenever anyone cries, "Wolf!" However, in an artificial environment where most of the "wolf" cries are false, the yogi will probably save himself a lot of bother – and ulcers – if he does not heed the warning. A certain amount of "cool-headedness" may also be beneficial even in a physical encounter with the danger. So the yogi's state of mind might, under certain circumstances, be a real improvement on nature.

V. *Non-attachment*

The direct activation of the pleasure circuit has a profound effect not only on memory but also on motivation. The choice of objects of motivation is made not only based on the stimuli presented, but also in terms of past experiences in similar circumstances. Desires rise up from the depths of the unconscious in a way similar to that discussed for negative experiences: "I want this candy because my grandmother used to always give me those; because I like everything that tastes sweet; because I have seen this beautiful model seductively devour the candy in a T.V. ad; because it is something pleasant to do, even though I am not really hungry." These elements of subconscious motivation will presumably be eradicated when the aim of all desire is achieved through the direct experience of ultimate bliss. An ancient Chinese scripture, *Sutra of Hui Neng*, says:

If we allow our thoughts, the past, the present and the future ones, to link up in a series, we put ourselves under restraint. On the other hand, if we let our mind attach to nothing at all times and towards all things, we gain emancipation. For this reason, we take 'Non-attachment' as our fundamental principle (Pine, 2013).

Man, however, is not a simple stimulus-response machine whose memories, activated by environmental inputs, prompt him into action. He is an "operant" agent, actively exploring his environment in search of satisfaction. This process of exploration, while advantageous regarding natural selection, is futile in terms of lasting or complete self-satisfaction.

As must be obvious, direct activation of the pleasure centres will "short-circuit" this search for pleasure based on past conditioning. Why strive and search when a high level of inner satisfaction has already been achieved? Does this mean that the enlightened man will lapse into a Buddhist state of "Nirodha" (a state of consciousness supposedly higher than Nirvana) with complete cessation of awareness and only enough physical activity maintained to be distinguished from a corpse? Some of the animal research may be interpreted to point in this direction. In some experiments, animals that were allowed to self-stimulate the pleasure centres continuously did so until they collapsed from exhaustion. They also disregarded such objects of reward as food, drink, and sex. However, some of the more thorough research modify this picture (Olds, 1956, pp. 105–116). In one long-term study it was found that even at the highest response rate (the highest degree of pleasure obtained), the animals were able to regulate their self-stimulation behaviour in a manner which was similar to the satisfaction of any other drive, such as hunger or thirst. In other words, when the animals had had enough, they went away and occupied themselves with other things. This possibly indicates that even continuous activation of the pleasure circuit will not disrupt the normal mode of satisfaction of our basic physiological drives. But the endless discontentment might cease.

There is no doubt that the religious mystics have discovered the truth about the ultimate futility of sense gratification. They knew that the only thing it does for certain is to bring pain and sorrow in its wake. Those who have discovered a superior means of unfailing *inner* gratification tried vainly to tell others that "the Kingdom of Heaven is within," and that they should, therefore "lay not up for themselves treasures upon earth." This injunction, needless to say, fell upon deaf ears. Most people were unable to realize that "the Kingdom of Heaven within" is not a mere metaphor, but a fact. The most they were able to derive from this teaching was a sense of disillusionment with the ephemeral world of sensuous pleasures. From this intellectual disillusionment the dogma of "renunciation" was born, conveniently **summarized for us by St. John of the Cross** (Steuart, 1999):

> In order to arrive at having pleasure in everything,
> Desire to have pleasure in nothing.
> In order to arrive at possessing everything,
> Desire to possess nothing.
> In order to arrive at knowing everything,
> Desire to know nothing.
> For
> When the mind dwells upon anything,
> Thou art ceasing to cast thyself upon the All.
> For, in order to pass from the all to the All
> Thou hast to deny thyself wholly in all.

Yet the "desires of the senses" could not be completely suppressed. At best, they were all sublimated into one huge, throbbing desire – "to find God." This desire is, naturally, still subject to all the laws affecting any other desire. In other words, it keeps the person in a state of constant search and discontentment: every attainment on the "path to God" is found to be an illusion. The frustrating search continues until the "seeker" falls into a ritualistic routine, very similar to that of an ordinary person who also warily gave up his search for his ultimate gratification through more gadgets or indulging in sex. The fate of the "ritual-mongers" is aptly described in the Indian scripture *Mundakopanishad* (Mead, 2010):

> Tottering variously under ignorance, yet
> boasting 'we alone are wise and learned'.
> fools ramble about suffering multifariously.
> like the blind led by the blind. Living
> diversely though within the fold of ignorance,
> these childish people pride themselves thinking
> that they have achieved the end of their life.

Subjected to passion and attachment, the ritual-mongers gain not true knowledge, and hence come back sorrow-stricken when the fruits of their deeds are exhausted.

Perhaps some of the first followers may have even tried to retrace the steps of their leader by doing exactly what he did to obtain the same results. This would not work for reasons that must now be obvious, and the experiences they would gain through their practices would be, at best, marginal. So they would begin to concentrate more and more on the dogmatic and ritualistic side of the leader's teaching. While the leader is still alive, this tendency would be kept in check with the leader realizing the tremendous gap existing between himself and his followers, and being aware that as soon as he dies they will distort his teaching out of all recognition, and in this way "betray" him.

This indeed seems to have inevitably happened in the case of all religions and cults. The irrelevant trappings of their leader's conversion, his necessarily ambiguous parable-laden pronouncements have become objects of uncritical reverence, bitter competition, theological disputes, and finally, violence. As anthropologist Weston La Barre points out in his monumental study of the origins of religion, "There is no mystery about religion. The genuine mysteries lie in what religion *purports to be about*...but religion itself is the beliefs, behaviours, and feelings of people." (La Barre, 2010, p. 1).

It will not have escaped the notice of the reader that we have dealt only with a small proportion of the practices and methods used by people to obtain the "spiritual benefits." Ordinary prayer, contemplation on some such subject as "I am in God, and He is in me," and the entire gamut of various other practices have not been touched upon. The reason for this is simple: unless these practices can do something to what appears to be the central problem of man, which is the conflict between his newly acquired thinking capacity and his old mechanisms of memory, emotion and motivation, they are somewhat irrelevant. This does not mean that they are entirely valueless. The ritual of prayer may bring people in the village together and create an atmosphere for social cohesion needed to fight off nature or hostile neighbours. The dogma may serve as a basis for a mutual consensus of opinion which, though not very meaningful in itself, saves people the trouble of inventing their own dogmas with all the inevitable hierarchical jockeying and the violence it entails.

To take another example, the practice of constantly reminding oneself that "I am in Him and He is in me" (or "mindful awareness" or any other "witnessing" technique), although it may not be effective in bringing about a Nirvana-like state, may have beneficial side effects. Firstly, it gives the individual a purpose in life, a sense of mastery over his destiny. Probably the greatest psychological handicap from which thinking man suffers is the hidden or acknowledged appreciation of the meaninglessness of his existence. Anything at all that will assuage this aimless feeling, no matter how irrational or primitive may be of value. Secondly, on a more technical level, the constant focusing of one's attention on an irrelevant point of reference could mechanically disrupt the ordinary processes of perception, memory and motivation and may therefore accidentally alleviate some of its worst defects. The effect would be similar to having, for example, a pin painfully stuck into one's body (one immediately thinks of the recluse's habit woven from rough camel hair), or being in a constant state of intoxication, with all the possible beneficial and deleterious effects such procedures may have on one's behaviour and rapport with the world.

However, mindfulness meditation, done properly, can also be viewed as means of "global desensitization" of stress embedded in the brain and the body (Valenstein, 1973, p. 172). Done over an extended period, it can lead to a more tranquil way of being and doing. The mind learns how to periodically tune-in onto the built-in gyroscope of peacefulness and rest inside the human brain – and stay there most of the time.

Chapter 3.
Modern Messiahs

I have selected a few examples of modern gurus who have been found to be representative of the broad range of philosophies. The analyses are not descriptive, but are "in-depth" in nature, and concern themselves mainly with the consciousness-modifying aspects of a particular teaching. Even though some opinions expressed may be judged as rather emphatic, they naturally spring from the author's ideas and personal experience and are not intended to discourage anyone from investigating these philosophies and practices personally.

I. J. Krishnamurti

There is probably no other writer who has placed the blame for man's misfortunes so squarely and uncompromisingly at the doorstep of man's neocortical thinking capacity as Jiddu Krishnamurti. To him, "thought" is the ultimate mischief-maker. "Thought," he writes, "in thinking about past pain or pleasure, gives continuity to it, sustains and nourishes it" (Krishnamurti, 2001, p. 21). Without studying the evolutionary background of man's thinking capacity, Krishnamurti is aware that there is "good" thought and "bad" thought. The thought that helps one to avoid danger or build a bridge is obviously "good." The thought which projects past fears into the future, fans desire, or creates division among men on ideological grounds is "bad." So, Krishnamurti explicitly asks a question on how to eliminate the abuses of thought without eliminating its uses. "Can thought," he writes, "completely operate in one direction and be totally silent in another so that it does not create a division?" (ibid. 1973, p. 462).

Jiddu Krishnamurti 1972
(photograph by Mary Zimbalist © The Estate of Mary Zimbalist)

Krishnamurti also traces the problem to memory. The conscious mind is nothing but the memory of the past. He maintains that what we ordinarily call "thinking" is actually nothing more than the automatic computer-like response of conscious and subconscious memories to environmental influence. A thought is always old. We walk around like robots, trying to answer the challenges of the present with the collection of memory residues of events long dead. Yet again, there are two kinds of memory – the "factual" and the "psychological." We want to retain the memory of how to build a bridge, but not the memory of past insults or past pleasures, which stop us from reacting adequately to the present.

What Krishnamurti is talking about becomes much clearer when we realize that when he talks about "psychological" memory or "psychological" (as opposed to chronological) time, he means "emotional" memory, time, etc. A thought is alright if it is not automatically tied to the collection of past *emotional* (and therefore physiological) experiences recorded by the memory. When it is on a purely abstract, disembodied level, it is a useful repository of facts; it leaves us the freedom to act spontaneously in the present. When thought is tied down to emotional memories, it has an unlimited capacity to generate imaginary fears and desires based on those memories, *The First and last Freedom* (Krishnamurti, 1969, p. 99).

Thus, the thought which has helped to achieve security in the past will attempt to maintain it and, by the very fact of trying to do so, create millions of imaginary and intangible fears. The "known" is the past memory record. The "unknown" is the product of the runaway capacity of the conceptual thought to generate all sorts of possibilities, both pleasant and unpleasant, based on the "known." This is how the fear of the "unknown" is born, for images of the "unknown" are inextricably connected to the past fearful memories of the "known." We have had some pain and illness, and the memory of it will create an incipient eternal fear of the repetition of this traumatic experience (Debenham et al. 1941, pp. 107-109).

The same thing happens with pleasant experiences. The memory of them will create a desire for their repetition. Krishnamurti is aware of the dual nature of the search for satisfaction. He says: "Being dissatisfied with one particular object of desire, we find a substitute for it. We are everlastingly moving from one object of desire to another which we consider being higher, nobler, more refined; but, however refined, desire is still desire, and in this movement of desire there is an endless struggle, the conflict of the opposites." This endless search is spurred by [the neocortical] "symbols, pictures, and images." In contrast to these insatiable desires there are physical *needs* – food, clothing, shelter, etc. – which are natural and can, most of the time, be easily satisfied on a purely physical level.

So how does one unhinge one's thought from one's emotional memories? By attaining stillness of the mind, says Krishnamurti. But how can one make the mind still? The mind cannot be *made* still, insists Krishnamurti. Any force, any effort in attempting to bring about the stillness of the mind is only going to bring about further conflict and distortion. So, meditation and "all the tricks of Yoga" are no good, for they all entail effort, conditioning and discipline. So what is one to do? The analysis does not help because it involves time, which still keeps us in the vicious circle of anticipated gratification, imagining and memory. Be "choicelessly aware" of the activities of your mind, says Krishnamurti, then through this process of extraordinary thoughtfulness, the mind will see its power of creating illusion and will go beyond. One asks oneself an impossible question: "How to expose the completely hidden content of the mind with all its trickery *"at one glance,"* without time, practice and analysis? When the thinking mind sees the immensity of this task and faces its logical impossibility, it just caves in. It "empties itself of everything." It has "exposed all the content of itself by denying the content."

"The sound of one hand clapping". (Fiantsev, 2017e)

Here, one immediately sees an undeniable similarity of Krishnamurti's approach and the Zen Buddhist "koan" practice. "Koan" is, after all, "impossible question" one asks of oneself and the flash of true understanding, the "Satori," occurs when the mind fully sees its incapacity to understand the "koan" on a logical thinking level. Those who think that this "enlightenment" is some particularly clear but still "normal" understanding should not delude themselves. What Krishnamurti talks about is a specific state of mind, even of the brain cells – a different dimension of which there is no description. This transformation profoundly alters even the seemingly immutable functions of the mind. The brain becomes just a useful recording instrument which serves, but no longer deludes the individual. Dreaming, which was a process of sorting out unresolved conflicts and expectations, becomes obsolete: there is literally "nothing to dream about."

The operation of the human mind in the manner that Krishnamurti finds objectionable is of course solidly wired into the human brain – and for good evolutionary reasons. If it was possible for a human being to see the whole content of his memory "at a glance," it would have probably resulted in irreversible psychosis. Even a partial opening of subconscious memory stores during some "bad" drug trips or psychotic episodes can be so shattering that the individual may never quite recover from it. The "understanding" that Krishnamurti is talking about is "pure understanding." It is achieved in some people with particularly permeable neurophysiological circuitry (usually caused by some form of epilepsy or a related disorder) that allows an occasional cross-talk to the limbic areas, which contain circuits capable of producing the sensations of "pure understanding." This perception is non-contextual and can be attached to whatever idea was dominant in mind at the moment of cross-talk (the "koan," "an impossible question," etc.). This cross-talk can be facilitated by tiring the neocortical circuitry with constant "mindfulness" or "choiceless awareness." As in meditation on a meaningless mantra, "choiceless awareness" implies the lack of neocortical associations, judgments, ideas, etc. When the conscious mind finally gives up its attempts to find the answer to the "impossible question," it enters, in extreme cases, a state of "ultraparadoxical" inhibition, described below in the discussion of Primal Therapy. As Pavlov suggested, man's thinking mind (the "secondary signalling system," in his terminology), being evolutionarily younger, is very likely to pass into the inhibitory stages with even relatively mild, but persistent bombardment by repetitive stimuli.

Similarly, immediate results were achieved by preachers like Wesley, who deliberately drove his listeners, through alternate promises of eternal damnation and salvation, into acute states of the collapse of their conscious thinking faculties. Wesley, like Krishnamurti, was also emphatic that "sanctification" comes either instantaneously, or not at all. He wrote that during his whole career he has not encountered a single person in whom sanctification was not an "instantaneous work."

Even the Indian epic *The Bhagavad Gita* (Prabhupada, 1989, p. 183) describes the enlightenment of its hero, the famous archer Arjuna, in terms reminiscent of instantaneous conversion under conditions of extreme stress. Arjuna's mind and heart are in deep conflict about the necessity of fighting the members of his clan which is his duty as a warrior, and his personal devotion to many of his potential adversaries. This produces in him a state of mental confusion, very much resembling the states of autonomic disarray that usually precede radical de-conditioning. His "limbs fail him," his "mouth is parched," his "body quivers," and his "hair stands on end." He cannot hold his bow properly and his skin is burning all over; his mind whirls and he is barely able to stand. Finally, after prolonged arguing with Lord Krishna, who is both his charioteer and spiritual adviser, Arjuna's conscious mind gives up. He declares himself utterly confused and feebleminded and entreats the Lord to "tell him what is good for him." Finding Arjuna in this suggestive state of utter submission, Krishna relents and instantaneously enlightens him. All the contradictions in Arjuna's mind are resolved in a state of cosmic unity.

There is little doubt that Krishnamurti's "enlightenment" in 1922 (which he called "the process") had all the hallmarks of a fully blown mystical experience, but with a host of epilepsy-like somatic reactions, such as pain, discomfort, spontaneous babbling, child-like states and a feeling of "otherness," culminating in a climatic experience of "immense peace".

Because Krishnamurti's "technique" is much gentler than that of either Wesley or Krishna, it can only be expected that the more powerful varieties of the experience he suggests will happen only in those rare individuals who have a good capacity for spontaneous cross-talk. For the vast majority of people, being "choicelessly aware" means just plain getting bored. In terms of being "enlightened", it could be an utter waste of time, as no doubt many followers of Krishnamurti have found out to their great chagrin. For some less lucky individuals, it may be a beginning of a psychotic episode. There is no guarantee at all that the inhibition of cortical activity through exhaustion is going to activate just the part of the limbic circuitry that we want. It obviously happened in the case of Krishnamurti himself, probably at an early stage in his life. For others it may not be "pure understanding" – it may be "pure pain."

Judging from questions and dialogues during Krishnamurti's talks, he is misunderstood not only on the deep level of "inner understanding," but also on a purely intellectual level. His differentiation of "psychological" and "physical" needs, memory, time, etc. is unclear to most people and his use of words like "knowledge" can be misleading and can easily provoke an ordinary person's intellectual resistance (e.g. in such cryptic phrases as "knowledge and learning are an impediment to understanding"). At times, Krishnamurti gets quite exasperated with his "thick skulled" listeners.

> Questioner: You said...
>
> Krishnamurti: No Sir, I did not say that. I did not say that. I will not go back through all that again – it is useless. You see, you will not face the actuality, the "what is!" You want to live in concepts, and I do *not* want to live in concepts. For Heaven's sake: love is not a concept. And because you have no love, you live in concepts. (And you all shake your heads, agree, and go on with your habits.) So why do you listen, why do you come here, because when we talk about these real things you are off – away at some tangent! Unfortunately, or fortunately, the speaker has talked for forty-two years. And when it comes to the point – which is to live without envy – you are not there!

Krishnamurti even unselfconsciously slips into a typically Zen way out of total intellectual stalemate by exclaiming in desperation: "if I hit you, you will *know* about that!" (Zen masters are reported to have struck their pupils and even chopped off their fingers to break down their pupils' intellectual defences.)

However, Krishnamurti may be comforted by the knowledge that all "spontaneous transcenders" (especially if their transformation happened at an early stage and they subsequently never acquired the clear understanding of the operation of "normal" consciousness) suffer from this lack of understanding by others. In fact, this misunderstanding can exist not only among the "enlightened" and the mere mortals but also among those who supposedly obtained their enlightenment by different means. A classic example of this is the famous 8th century "Quietist controversy" between the Indian Buddhist School that taught gradual realization through a precise number of clearly defined steps and the Chinese Zen School, which taught "sudden Enlightenment." The views of the main exponent of the latter school, Ho-shan, are, in fact, very similar to those of Krishnamurti. A confrontation between the spokesmen of these two schools was arranged. It was significant by its total absence of meaningful communication between the two representatives.[k]

To sum up, Krishnamurti's analysis of the predicament of man is valuable, but only if one understands his ambiguous terminology. His other main contribution is his just and incisive criticism of the many traditional approaches to the problem. His own solution appears to be applicable only to a few earnest and peculiarly endowed individuals who can persevere in tiring their intellectual capacities in the absence of the traditional guidance and reinforcement (such as those developed by Zen schools (Livingston, pp. 574-575) to the level of their complete exhaustion which will trigger off, hopefully, just the right kind of subcortical response.

II. Transcendental Meditation (TM)

Transcendental Meditation (TM) technique is easier to analyze than most others because it has been subjected to quite an unprecedented amount of independent scientific scrutiny, and also because its main exponent, Maharishi

---

[k] Many of Krishnamurti's dialogues with other thinkers are now on YouTube. Those who wish to read examples from such fascinating exercises in non-communication can do so in the "Buddhist Scriptures".

Mahesh Yogi (1969) presents a fairly clear and unambiguous picture of his teaching.

The theoretical foundation of TM is based on a new interpretation of the sacred Indian scripture The *Bhagavad Gita*. Maharishi Mahesh Yogi also maintains that his teaching springs directly from the most ancient Indian scriptural writings – the Vedas. Once again, the essence of these teachings is claimed to have been misinterpreted and misunderstood for countless ages, with the current exponent setting out to put the record straight.

Maharishi Mahesh Yogi
(photograph by Bahgavan, © Sri Ramanasramam)

To anyone who reads The *Bhagavad Gita* with an impartial eye, it will be immediately clear that it was written by someone who advocated the traditional Indian approach to renunciation – withdrawal of the senses, abstinence from bad habits, etc. – as a *path* to realization, and not as a *result* of it. The verse, "For an undisciplined man, Yoga is hard to achieve, so I consider; but it can be gained through proper means by the man of endeavour who is disciplined," can mean only one thing: *Yoga is a hard grind*. It is difficult to see how something as straightforward as this can be misinterpreted, as Maharishi insists.

Nobody can misinterpret what Maharishi (Yogi, 2001) says in this respect. His teaching is unequivocal: do not put the cart before the horse; no practice of the virtues will get one anywhere until one has repeated experiences of Bliss-consciousness, which will make those virtues part of one's nature. Until that experience is achieved, forced practice of the virtues will only mean strain and hypocrisy. It is a pity that Maharishi tried to force this lively bit of wisdom into the Procrustean scriptural bed. His commentary on some verses (Maharishi, 1968, ch 6, vers. 10, 13, 35, 45) amounts to a virtual distortion of the original text. One understands, of course, that for an Indian to claim that he (or his tradition) has come up with something new is simply inconceivable. Everything must hark back to the Ancient Scriptures to be of any value (Conze, 1959, pp. pp. 214-7).

The message Maharishi brings out is indeed in vivid contrast to most spiritual guidance: meditation, he says, should be fun. The mind wants, by itself, to go in the direction of greater bliss. Give it a suitable medium on which to focus its attention, and it will begin its march towards the source of thought, which is also the source of bliss. It will be noticed that the mantras given to beginners in TM are meaningless one or two syllable words, which should, at least in theory, be able to generate the fast "cross-talk frequencies." In TM, the process of meditation is defined as, "turning the attention inwards towards the subtler levels of a thought until the mind transcends the experience of the subtlest state of the thought and arrives at the source of the thought." Greater bliss and relaxation accompany the perception of the subtler levels of thought. Using our terminology, it can be said that the gently pulsing mantra creates the "cross-talk" effect and activates a more direct circuitry to the pleasure centres. This circuitry, as pointed out earlier, is probably similar to that utilized for indirect reward procurement through the satisfaction of our ordinary needs (sex, food, etc.).

It has been observed that during TM the dominant alpha frequencies (8-13 Hz), supposedly associated with states of relaxation and pleasure, gradually shift forward, towards the frontal areas (one can say, roughly in the direction of the pleasure centres).

Occasionally, and usually, with more experienced meditators, trains of theta waves appear in the frontal leads. Theta waves (4-7 Hz) have been termed "the pleasure scanners." In an ingenious experiment by Grey Walter (who coined the above term), a male subject was stroked by an attractive female assistant while the EEG record was being taken. As soon as she stopped stroking, trains of theta waves occurred ("please keep doing this, I like it"). It was also noticed that in meditation both cerebral hemispheres become quickly engaged in a highly synchronized rhythmical alpha activity.

This may suggest that as the mantra is allowed to join the limbic reward circuit (the frequencies of short TM-type mantras were found to be in the theta range) the focus of nervous activity shifts toward the frontal and deeper areas of the brain. The synchronously functioning cerebral hemispheres begin to resemble a twin resonator for the more powerful activity that occurs in the limbic system. The processes of "unstressing," desensitization, and increased pleasure and relaxation can then theoretically occur.

Here we also have the elements of an extremely subtle built-in biofeedback system. The pulsating mantra adjusts its frequency to "feed through" into the conscious brain the maximum amount of pleasurable "seepage." The diminution of inputs from the environment (closing the eyes, assuming a relaxed posture) and from the cerebral hemispheres (absence of coherent thinking, lack of conscious associations with the mantra) will facilitate the activation of the subcortical limbic circuitry. Once "the seepage" of pleasurable sensations directly from the pleasure centres has begun, the process of meditation becomes truly effortless. The powerful pull of the bliss areas is sufficient to keep the attention glued to it.

Maharishi emphasized the element of non-interference with the natural tendency of the mind to go in the direction of greater bliss. Any conscious effort or analysis will not only impede the progress of attention towards the source of bliss but may even bring some undesirable sensations. The attention that has already begun to penetrate the deep non-verbal limbic circuitry is apt to stray into areas that may provoke adverse reactions. Maharishi issues a clear warning about the negative influence of conscious interference with the meditation process:

> The intensity of thought is very great at that subtle level of thinking where the mind is slipping out of thought and is about to lose the experience of the relative field. If the process is not disturbed and is allowed to go by itself in a very innocent manner, then the mind slips into the Self. If on the other hand, pressure or force is applied in any way to check the mind or to control the process, the mind will be thrown off the course on which it is

naturally set and off-balance into agitation and a feeling of discomfort.

If this rule is followed, supposedly nothing untoward can happen. Left to itself, the attention has no inclination to deviate onto any other path except the path of greater bliss. The principle "no peace – no bliss" is clearly delineated by Maharishi. The degree of peace necessary for perception of ultimate bliss is truly remarkable. In meditation, the breath "becomes more refined and eventually comes to a standstill." However, the full attainment of this peculiar physiological state of "restful alertness" is initially impossible. As the body attains greater degrees of restfulness it tends to throw off some "strain in the nervous system." This strain will manifest itself as thought and will push the attention back to the surface level of the mind. Only gradually will the blissful nature of the Self be infused into the ordinary consciousness. The thoughts that arise during meditation should be disregarded; one should simply go back to one's mantra and proceed with meditation "in a relaxed way."

In general, Maharishi's attitude toward conscious thought is very similar to Krishnamurti's. "Transcending thought," he writes, "is infinitely more valuable than thinking." A thought is intimately implicated in the production of "insatiable desires." The abstract thought springs from the mind and develops into a real desire based on past impressions, which are the "seed of desire that leads into action." This action will, in turn, create a memory to serve as a seed of future action. Thus, man is bound to a cycle of impression, desire, and action that keeps him acting in a puppet-like fashion. The natural forces ("the gunas of Nature") employ man's consciousness as a stage for their interplay, while he mistakenly assumes the authorship of his action.

The desire for fleeting joys, prompted by thought, can only lead to sorrow, "there being no point in relativity to satisfy finally its craving for greater happiness." Maharishi's answer to this problem of perpetual frustration and discontentment is not to control or reduce the desire, but to fully satisfy it by reaching a state of permanent inner Bliss-consciousness. In that state, even though the mind still entertains thoughts, they do not exert any binding influence upon the individual. His senses are sharper than before, as the constant anxiety and the resultant stress have been lifted, but the experience of the sensory pleasures fails to create an emotional memory, which would serve as a seed for future action and involvement. The individual's consciousness is too dominated by the perception of inner bliss to register sensory impressions. The binding cycle of impression, desire, and action has been cut asunder.

From a neurophysiological viewpoint, it is conceivable that a circuit as powerful as that, connecting cortical awareness to the pleasure centres, would change the customary motivation and memory traffic. Cortical motivation will no longer have a binding influence because the "carrot" which was used to lure it along is now freely available at any time. The emotional memories have been neutralized through the process of "unstressing" during meditation. The physical state of the body has also been changed. The state of calmness, which was at first experienced only during meditation itself, tends to become more and more persistent. At first, exposure to activity would shatter the inner peace, but repeated exposures would "harden" it, not unlike the way in which the colour of a piece of cloth becomes fast after it has been alternatively exposed to the sun and dipped in the dye. **As Maharishi succinctly summarizes:** "Self-awareness acts as a shock-absorber on the mental level, while the state of restful alertness of the nervous system acts as a shock-absorber on the physical level." Neurophysiologically it is conceivable again that the powerful parasympathetic activity, provoked through the direct activation of the pleasure centres, will be superimposed upon whatever activity the body is engaged in. Its superimposition upon the ordinary sympathetic/parasympathetic oscillation will produce a peculiar physiological state. The constant background of calmness throughout all types of activities makes it organically impossible for a "fight or flight" memory to be effectively filed. The "hypothalamic tuning" is permanently on the "calm" mode, which desensitizes painful or overly exciting memories.

Maharishi himself explains the relaxation, which accompanies the process of meditation as a result of the diminution of physical activity, and that is proportionate to the diminution of mental activity produced by a perception of the mantra on a more "refined" and subtle level of thinking. This could be another way of saying that, as the mantra regresses towards subcortical and non-verbal levels, it is perceived as becoming "finer." As the appropriate "restful" circuitry also becomes activated during this process, the physical activity correspondingly diminishes. Alertness also seems to go together with the restfulness and pleasure. Heath (1964, p. 224) in his human experiments with implanted electrodes noted, "with septal stimulation the patients brightened, looked more alert, and seemed to be more attentive to their environment during, and for at least a few minutes after, the period of stimulation."

As Krishnamurti Maharishi claims that the new level of consciousness profoundly alters not only waking but also dreaming and sleeping stages. The attractiveness of bliss-consciousness is such that in time it is maintained uninterruptedly, "through all the activity of the waking and dreaming states and through the silence of the deep sleep state." It is true that in our primitive brains there are centres that maintain awareness around the clock. A typical example quoted is that of a mother who will sleep soundly through the noise of heavy traffic but will immediately wake up when the baby stirs or cries. There must be some centre in the brain that was maintaining "watchful alertness" all the time.

The attainment of permanent Bliss-consciousness (or "Cosmic-consciousness"), which would be regarded as many as a pinnacle of personal evolution, is looked upon by Maharishi as only a half-way house to the ultimate state of "Unity." In a sense, cosmic consciousness highlights the duality between the permanent nature of the Self and the impermanence of the manifest world as perceived by the senses. As Maharishi puts it: "The eyes cannot see Being, the tongue cannot taste It, the ears cannot hear, nor the hands touch It." The state of consciousness has been changed, but the separation of the inner Being from the world of gross material phenomena is still felt. At this stage, the notion of Yogic Union/Samadhi finally becomes relevant: now there is something to unite. This is accomplished through the conscious practice of "the most refined activity of all, the activity of devotion to God," when "everything is naturally experienced in the awareness of God."

Love and reverence. (Fiantsev, 2017f)

It is fascinating to speculate about the possible neurophysiological substratum of this state of consciousness (if it indeed exists, as Maharishi and other mystics claim). The emotions of love and reverence are continuously cultivated in one's transactions with the world. Gradually, the traffic that carries the emotions of love and reverence becomes an inseparable part of the unified (and blissful) perception of the world. It is also possible that at this point a neural area deals with the sensations of "unity" is directly activated.[1]

The adjective "pure," which Maharishi attaches to the various aspects of the transcendent perception ("pure awareness," "pure bliss," "pure intelligence," "pure

---

[1] A psychotic case where the borderline between the self and the world has been loosened (such as in a schizophrenic who mutilates his body to harm his enemies) lends some indirect support to this idea. But it is also true that sensations of pure "Unity" are coded in the human brain and in rare cases may be accessed and even integrated into consciousness.

creativity," etc.), confirms the earlier expressed notion that in the human brain there are areas that house undiluted perceptions, which are similar to, but much stronger than, those of ordinary awareness. The situation here is similar to that found in the use of drugs and creativity. Whether the "expansion of consciousness" or "tapping the creative source of thought" in TM can have any direct influence on creativity is something which may need further investigation by impartial observers. So far, none of TM'ers has come up with any Nobel-prize material.

Even though TM appears to utilize the physiological mechanisms favouring transcendence in the human brain, all the qualifications that have been discussed in relation to the relative inaccessibility of higher states of consciousness to ordinary (non-epileptic) people would, naturally, apply here as well. It is said that Maharishi used to indicate that five years of regular meditation should be enough to take one to the level of "Cosmic consciousness." By now, literally tens thousands of people should be "cosmically conscious" and dwelling in "pure bliss," if Maharishi's estimate was correct, enjoying the tremendous energy and creativity that were open in the past only to a few selected saints and savants. Yet, this hope, like the hope of initiating 1% of the world population into TM during the first ten years of preaching TM, proved to be grossly overoptimistic. The literature, which emanates from the Maharishi University of Management (MUM) that should supposedly have the concentration of these people with highly expanded consciousness is amazingly unimaginative and intellectually simplistic. It seems to be dominated by Maharishi's curious blend of clichéd Western science and refurbished Vedic mysticism put into scientific-sounding jargon.

The attempt by Maharishi to stimulate the dwindling interest in his technique by announcing his extraordinary claims of miraculous capabilities for TM practitioners resulted in discrediting the cult among all serious observers, which accelerated its descent into obscurity. It even led to some former disciples bringing a lawsuit against the cult, saying that after spending tens of thousands of dollars, they have only learned to hop on battered mattresses, and not levitate in the air.

III. Primal Therapy

Arthur Janov, the inventor of the "Primal," summarizes the basis for his approach to dealing with neurological disorders in these words:

Painful and unacceptable messages are organized below the level of conscious awareness; the body reacts to a pain of which it is unaware, and this pain sets in motion a lifetime of behaviours involving flight, both mentally and physically (Janov, 1972, p. 45).

The major painful traumas are designated by Janov as the "Primal Scenes" and his therapeutic approach is directed at them:

The reliving of that Primal Scene will produce violent thrashing, even convulsive behaviour, just because it unleashes *all* of the early terror. Experiencing that tower of terror is earthshaking and, in my opinion, curative, because it was the suppression of the fear which produced neurotic behaviour (ibid).

Janov presents this theory as a fundamental breakthrough in the understanding of mental illness and indeed of human psychology in general. To anyone even vaguely familiar with psychoanalytical notions it will immediately become clear that Janov has simply restated, in the guise of new terminology and in a dramatic form, the general tenets of psychoanalysis. The subconscious memories became "Primal Pain," the major repressed traumatic experiences became "Primal Scenes,"[m] the Freudian "abreaction" (release of repressed memories) – the "Primal." Janov, however, firmly disassociates himself from psychoanalysis, which he regards as ineffective. He sees the major cleavage between himself and psychoanalysis to be that traditional psychoanalytic treatment makes the patient simply "explain" his repressed feelings, whereas Primal therapy makes him "relive" them. In other words, Janov emphasizes inability to act out one's "natural" impulses as a major cause of the future neurotic behaviour and places great importance upon retrospective acting out of repressed memories during the process of abreaction ("Primal").

First of all, it is not true that Freud, for one, did not realize the importance of suppressed bodily reactions during emotionally tense situations as a major cause of neurosis (Freud, 1955, pp. 153-230). In *Studies on Hysteria* (which he wrote together with Breuer), it is stated that the persistence of traumatic memory depended on many factors, the most important of which is "whether there has been an energetic reaction to the event that provokes an affect" (Breuer & Freud, 2000, pg. 8).

---

[m] In Freudian literature the terms "primal fantasy," "primal scene," etc. are limited to the child's observation (or fantasies) of parental intercourse.

"An energetic reaction" could be "crying one's self out," "blowing off steam," or even such a complex behavioural reaction as revenge.

Secondly, Freud and Breuer were aware that the release of pent-up aggression or any other emotion could be accomplished in a physical fashion long after the event that provoked it. They did this with the aid of hypnosis. In one particular case, a patient was made to relive, under hypnosis, a scene in which his employer had insulted and physically attacked him in the street. It turned out that the patient had already been reliving that experience, in fashion, through his hysterical fits, which comprised periods of uncontrollable rage. In other words, he was having spontaneous "Primals", and this was what brought him to a psychiatrist's office. The question arises: why did Freud, who realized the causative effects of repressed motor reactions and pent-up emotion in neurosis and could also provoke these reactions in a therapeutic setting, fail to put two and two together and leave it to Janov to inaugurate the "Primal Revolution" (a title of one of Janov's books)? The answer, I think, is simple – *Freud wanted to treat hysteria, not to encourage it.*

Primal scream. (Fiantsev, 2017g)

To elaborate: Firstly, Freud and Breuer recognized the tremendous therapeutical potential of language. They state quite explicitly that language serves as a substitute for action; and that through language an effect can be abreacted almost as effectively as through action itself. There can be no doubt about the fact that Freud and his colleagues were able to, through mere "explaining" (as Janov puts it), bring dramatic cures of a great number of neurotic patients. Words and language, through a chain of conscious/subconscious associations, ultimately lead to the sphere of emotion and feeling (Arnold, 1960, pp. 33-34). Thus, the reconnection between the intellect and emotion that Janov speaks about can be accomplished through "words alone." From the theories discussed in the previous chapters, this is a fragmented approach aimed at localized "complexes." There is no doubt, however, that it can be effective in bringing a maladjusted neurotic more into line with what we regard as normality.

Secondly, and perhaps more importantly, Freud and Breuer emphasized that emotional releases (like bursting into tears or breaking a vase instead of somebody's head) are not the only sane way of integrating one's feelings. The traumatic memory can be "diluted" and neutralized through the process of association with other ideas which have, in the past, given a person their sense of stability in their relationships with the outside world. "A person's memory of humiliation," they write, "is corrected by his putting the facts right, by considering his worth, etc. In this way, a normal person can bring about the disappearance of the accompanying effect through the process of association" (ibid. p. 9). There is little doubt that this commonsensical cognitive/behavioural procedure works well enough with most people most of the time. It may not neutralize emotional memories completely, but it can certainly prevent many of them from erupting into gross pathological symptoms.

If the traumatic memories that underlie neurosis have not been disposed of through the process of abreaction or by associative thought-activity, they lead to a hysterical fit. What does this fit comprise of? Freud and Breuer write:

> The motor phenomena of hysterical attacks can be interpreted partly as universal forms of reaction appropriate to the effect accompanying the memory (such as kicking about and waving the arms and legs, which even young babies do), partly as a direct expression of these memories (ibid. p. 15).

This is, of course, a very precise description of what Janov likes to represent as a "Primal." If there is still doubt in anyone's mind about the fact that Janov's "Primals" are nothing more than the classical hysterical fits, this doubt is dispelled by analysing the experience of the "Primal" as described by his patients. The following account is fairly typical:

> A great gale of frightening, horrible, terrifying, deadly pain begins to rise from my guts, up and up and up and nothing can hold it back as it finally explodes from my throat in a truly monstrous chain of piercing screams. I remember only little of it, except that it seemed to go on forever and that my whole body, every nerve and fibre of me, seemed to be involved in it, grotesquely convulsing and pulsating with the agony of it... Most astonishing of all, right in the middle of it I became very intrigued with a growing awareness that somewhere within me I was

also calmly, even happily, witnessing this with a certain amount of 'scientific' curiosity, wondering at the incredible amount of explosive power that I must have contained in my system all these years (Janov, 1972).

The "double consciousness" described here is, of course, one of the most typical symptoms of a hysterical outburst. The language in which this patient describes his experiences also betrays certain qualities of his character, which are ordinarily associated with hysteria. Here is Breuer's description of the alteration of consciousness during a hysterical fit, which he regards as "a universally known example of a division of psychical activity:"

At their beginning, conscious thought is often extinguished ["I remember only little of it"]; but afterwards, it gradually awakens. Many intelligent patients admit that their conscious ego was quite lucid during the attack and looked on with curiosity and surprise at all the mad things they did and said (Breuer & Freud, 2000).

An even more striking proof of the existence of "double-consciousness" in hysteria is provided by the 17th century English physician Edward Jorden (MacDonald, 2013):

A young Maiden also upon some passion of the mind, as it was credibly reported, fell into these fits of the Mother [hysteria], and being in one of them, a Physician then present modestly put his hand under her clothes to feel a windy tumour, which she then had in her back. However, a Surgeon there also present not contented with that manner of examination, offered to take up her clothes and to see it bare: whereupon the Maid being greatly offended, took such indignation at it, as it did put her presently out of her fit.

Although the similarity between what Janov describes as a "Primal" and a hysterical fit must be clear to anyone with even an elementary psychiatric understanding, Janov nowhere openly acknowledges it. In one place only, does he permit himself a slip of the tongue? He writes about the harm which the conventional methods of therapy do to a psychiatric patient and explains it in the following manner: "As soon as the patient gets 'hysterical,' that is, *as soon as he is on the verge of a Primal*, instead of helping him into that feeling, a chemical (or electrical shock therapy) lid is clamped on it, and the tension builds again." In another place, Janov's patient, quoting Freud, unselfconsciously reminds the reader about the "female hysteric whose attacks were an unmistakable imitation of the birth process."

The "Birth Primal" is, of course, one of the main pillars of Janov's therapy, and can significantly facilitate the rest of the therapy. To remember feelings such as "I am being drowned by birth liquid," a patient may be subjected to a simulated suffocation produced by wet towels wrapped around his head. The therapist may even "butt the person's head against a pillow or a wall." The aim of these "therapeutic" procedures, states Janov, "is to elicit early memory circuits." Hysterically predisposed patients, subjected to such treatment, predictably produce extremely vivid memories of birth, or whatever else is suggested to them. They report detailed feelings of "something" that was wrapped around their feet so that they could not move them freely (the mysterious "something" is, of course, readily identified as placenta).

According to Janov, another one of his patients performed an even more dazzling (literally and figuratively) feat of remembrance: during his "Birth Primal," he "felt blinded by the strong light in the delivery room." It is hard to say whether a newborn baby can differentiate between the light produced by an external source and, say, "photisms" produced by putting pressure on its eyelids. Probably not. Janov not only thinks that the baby already perceives an external light in a "room," but retains a traumatic memory of it which will, later in life, make him see flying saucers as "lights in the sky."[n]

An even more palpable proof of remembrance of things long past was produced by a female patient of Janov who brought with herself back from one of her "Birth Primals" a real-life birthmark, supposedly gone since just after birth. To anyone who has heard of hysterical "stigmata" (physical manifestations of emotional upheaval in hysterics) the true origin of the newly acquired birthmark must be clear. Medieval hysterics used to maintain that drops of blood, which appeared on their hands and feet, were a sufficient proof of Christ's crucifixion. Similar stigmata can be readily produced by a suggestion in deep hypnosis.

It would be interesting to know how many of Janov's patients have heard of Piaget's stages of development of cognitive capacities in children. The great Swiss developmental psychologist postulated definite stages in the growth of intellectual and perceptual capacity in children, which appear to be biologically determined and, as some unsuccessful attempts have shown, cannot be skipped. A baby under nine months of age, if presented with a bottle with its nipple turned away, will not attempt to grasp it, because its shape looks unusual and fails to recognize it. During the first two years of his life, the child still remains

---

[n] This is not to dispute that birth deliveries, as performed in most Western hospitals, may be psychologically damaging (Leboyer, 1975). What is disputed is the authenticity of their recall and the straightforward way in which they, according to Janov, affect adult behaviour.

largely "egocentric" (i.e. cannot place himself in the position of other people). One of Janov's patients, at the age of *six months*, was already capable of such profound intimations:

> As my lips shape themselves for her nipples, do not her nipples shape themselves for my lips? Mommy? As she is my food, am I not her hunger? Mommy? As I cry for her milk, does her milk not cry for me? Mommy? ... [Followed by a piercing cry of "Mommy! Mommy!]

How did it happen that Janov was able to present such an old-fashioned affliction as hysteria in the form of not only a new but *therapeutic* breakthrough? Firstly, one must realize that hysteria is an extraordinarily loose and flexible classification (Veith, 1965, p. 124). Looking historically at the manifestations of this disorder, one notices with surprise that after surviving for centuries under various guises ("possession by the Devil," "fits of the Mother," etc.) it practically disappeared in the past few decades. During Freud's time, it was a prevalent neurotic disorder. Then it had brief resurgences during the First and Second World Wars, only to disappear almost overnight from the contemporary scene. But had it? Freud and Breuer attributed the occurrence of a hysterical fit to a "hallucinatory reproduction of memory which was of importance in bringing about the onset of hysteria – the memory either of a single major trauma...or of a series of interconnected part-traumas." The underlying mechanism of the hysterical disorder was the "splitting of the mind into two relatively independent portions." This is exactly how Janov describes the causation of common neurosis and psychosis, only calling the "splitting of the mind" a "disconnection." Just as Janov views everyone as a potential neurotic, some early investigators viewed hysteria in the same fashion. H. Bernheim (1837-1919) of the famous Nancy School of Psychiatry suggested that hysteria was not really a disease but a syndrome and that everyone was potentially more or less hysterical.

However, what happened to all the "kicking about," "waving of the arms and legs," fainting, uncontrollable crying, and all the other motor phenomena, which gave hysteria its unmistakable character? A historian of this affliction Ilza Weith (1965) suggests an explanation:

> Unacceptable today would be the fainting ladies of the Victorian period, partly because they would altogether fail to evoke any sympathetic response in their social environment and partly because the skill of fainting gracefully has almost disappeared. With the increasing awareness of conversion reactions and the popularisation of psychiatric literature, the 'old-fashioned' somatic expressions of hysteria have become suspect among the more sophisticated classes and hence, most physicians observe that obvious conversion symptoms are now rarely encountered and, if at all, only among the uneducated of the lower social strata.

The particular forms which hysterical fits take are notoriously subject to contagion and imitation. An 18th century French physician described how a girl who was suffering from hysterical bouts of hiccups was placed in the same room with four other women who were afflicted by various other diseases. After being together for three days, all of them were simultaneously seized by violent attacks of hiccups and convulsions so severe that it required an effort of four men to hold down just one of them. As the Scottish physiologist and physician Robert Whytt (1714-1766) wryly observed, "This illness in which the women invent, exaggerate, and repeat all the different absurdities of which a disordered imagination is capable, is sometimes epidemic and contagious" (Whytt, 2013).

The mass hysterical reactions that occurred in the religious convents in the Middle Ages and the Renaissance are another well-known examples of the contagious nature of hysterical disorders. The incredible adaptability of hysterics had even fooled, at one time, such a thorough investigator of psychiatric disorders as Jean-Martin Charcot of the famous Salpétrieré Hospital in Paris. At one stage, hysterical patients were transferred into a ward of this hospital that already housed epileptics. This did not affect the epileptics, while the sufferers from hysteria began to mimic epileptic seizures and assume the famous "bizarre postures" of Charcot. A new name of "hystero-epilepsy" was given to this peculiar disease. Later, however, Charcot realized his mistake and withdrew the term.

It should hardly come to us as a surprise when we note that in Primal therapy the hysterical fits and their rationalization by the patients fall into highly stylised and stereotyped forms suggested by Janov's writings. Janov himself intimates that he and his "highly trained staff" use some sophisticated, almost mysterious techniques to evoke "Primals" in his patients. He gives away some clues, though, like the previously mentioned suffocation with wet towels, hitting the head against a wall, or surrounding the patient with toys, playpen, and childhood photos. A careful reading of the case histories quoted by Janov suggests, however, that at least some of his highly sensitive and hysteria-prone patients began "Primaling" almost before they introduced themselves at the reception desk in the clinic and certainly before they received any therapeutic guidance whatever.

The fundamental biological basis of neurosis is, according to Janov, a tendency of all forms of organic life to withdraw from pain. Thus, he sees the mechanism of repression as being a mere extension of that universal principle. The overwhelming "Primal Pains," such as rejection by one's parents, cannot be integrated into normal consciousness which "withdraws" from them. The repressed traumatic memory is kept in a nervous "reverberating circuit" which causes the organism to maintain a constant state of tension, forcing it to re-channel this energy into neurotic behaviour. Janov even views the evolutionary growth of the human neocortex as a possible result of the repression that became necessary when organized society began to "trample" the individual's feelings under its restrictive concepts of "respect," "reverence," "loyalty," and "obedience." Janov seems to subscribe to the traditional myth of the "Noble Savage" when he says, "the deforming of natural man [by society] is the beginning of human destruction."

There are two flaws implicit in Janov's theory. First, if the avoidance of pain is a universal biological phenomenon, then exactly how is a reversal of this principle in Primal therapy (making the patient feel the pain) beneficial to a human being? Secondly, there are good grounds to believe that the development of the human neocortex began long before the "repressive" society, as we understand it, came into being. Moreover, the "individual's feelings," as we learn now from ethnological studies, were always "trampled upon," in the animal kingdom.

For example, an adolescent male baboon must do a lot of "repressing" if he is to survive in aggressive encounters with dominant males. Like a human child, he has to put on an "appeasement grin" to avoid being severely punished by the elders. The life of the adolescent baboon on the fringe of the troop is the most psychologically trying and physically dangerous thing imaginable. The young males are the first ones to meet the teeth of the predator; this fate catches up with them even quicker when, in exceptional cases, they leave the troop in frustration and begin to roam on their own. Yet baboons, whose society would rank among the most restrictive known, have failed to show any progressive enlargement of the neocortex. The baboon troop, with its individual aggression subordinated to the needs of the collective, is one of the most effective societies with a survival potential much higher than that of the more intelligent apes (until relatively recent times, there were more baboons in Africa than people.) The reason for this becomes clear when one realizes that evolution pays its highest premium not for keeping the individual's tender feelings intact, but for preserving the regenerative potential of the individual and the troop. The entire social structure of the baboon evolved to give maximum protection to the very young and the females.

Another concept that Janov uses in his therapy is the myth of the insidious, diabolical, terrifying "Pain" (which he always respectfully writes as a proper noun) that is locked somewhere deep within his patients' systems only to break out when the right switches are pressed, into a convulsing orgy of their "Primals." Here Janov is treading a very well-worn path. In the medieval times, the "Pain" used to go under a much more homely and awe-inspiring designation of the "Devil" or "unholy powers." These powers caused the various bizarre manifestations of neuroses and psychoses – irrational fears, visions, loss of sight and hearing, insensitivity to pain, and terrible contortions. They could also be conveniently exorcised by an application of some formula such as: "Thou dumb and deaf spirit, I charge thee, come out of him, and enter no more into him." This would be followed by a "Primal:" "And the spirit cried, and rent him sore and came out of him."°

The therapeutic value of emotional collapse and subsequent psychological "release" was known and used throughout the world since time immemorial. Alberto Pirijano describes how African witch doctors treated a girl who suffered from melancholia, brought upon by a "dark and evil spirit" (Pirijano, 1955). She was required to dance in a frenzied fashion for many hours to the accompaniment of drums and rhythmic singing, until "a stream of foam and sweat ran down from the corners of her mouth." Then, with a "piercing shriek," she fell to the ground, after which the attendants repeatedly immersed her in water. When all this was finished, she, feeling obviously happy about the result of her treatment, "smiled ecstatically and cast her eyes heavenwards." Many more fascinating examples, some of them contemporary, are given in W. Sargant's book *The Mind Possessed* (Sargant & Walters, 1973).

Janov's fervent belief in the all-pervasiveness and power of "Pain" seems to match the zeal of the "Holy Fathers" who saw the Devil's influence in all human doing and attempted to expurgate it accordingly. To Janov, happiness is not a positive phenomenon – it is the "obverse of depression." The whole huge body of evidence which has been accumulated since the discovery of the pleasure centres in the human and animal brain is ignored by Janov. "The

---

° This Biblical description is generally thought to pertain to epilepsy, but the two diseases were often confused, and the above description fits hysteria just as well.

pursuit of happiness," he states, "is a neurotic endeavour of a body in pain and the mind in flight." In his book *The Anatomy of Mental Illness*, pleasure is not even listed in the index while various aspects of pain are accorded eighteen entries.

Janov in *The Anatomy of Mental Illness* (1971, p. 76) mentions experiments carried out at Tulane University Medical School on human subjects who had electrodes implanted into their brains. "These subjects," writes Janov, "were usually in intractable Pain." Out of 54 patients mentioned in the report, only six were in intractable pain. The majority of them were schizophrenics. The elimination of depression and anxiety, the immediate relief of pain and increased contentment were not due, as Janov says, to some vague "pain-suppressive functions of the limbic system." It was due to the stimulation of the *pleasure* centres in the brain. All the historical evidence of ecstatic experiences from St. Paul to Dostoyevsky is dismissed by Janov in one single phrase: "There is no super-ecstasy or 'peak' experience; these are neurotic notions."

Here, we come to the question of the "cures" observed in Primal therapy. The more fantastic subjective reports, such as those of promoted growth of previously stunted breasts and teeth, can be safely put into the category of "miraculous cures," which were frequently observed in hysterics during medieval times and which were probably due to suggestion and exaggeration. Other less specific subjective reports of psychological improvement cannot be, as Janov admits, taken at their face value due to the possibility of suggestion. Yet the objective data that emanates from "the fully equipped research laboratory at the Primal Institute in Los Angeles where research on patients proceeds day and night," is extremely scanty. In *The Anatomy of Mental Illness* book (1971) Janov reported a drop of anal temperature and some EEG and blood pressure changes. A year later in his *Primal Revolution* (1972, p. 45) and four years later in *Primal Man* he still had little news to report. It is obvious that any abreactive psychotherapeutic process is bound to produce *some* changes. It is equally obvious that the repeated series of hysterical convulsions are going to affect the physiological state of the body.

We may also wonder why Janov did not choose the more widely used psychological tests (e.g. Spielberger, Cattell, or Bendig's Anxiety Scales) to measure the level of tension and anxiety in his patients instead of the incredibly crude anal temperature. The psychological changes that Primal therapy produces could have been objectively measured by some widely used test as the Minnesota Multiphasic Personality Inventory. It is simply not enough to say nowadays that a therapy produces "a better, less demanding human being." We can, however, make a guess about the broad physiological effects of Primal therapy by looking at some research into identical therapeutic techniques.

To the best of my knowledge, Janov nowhere acknowledges that his method of treatment had direct predecessors in the form of attempts to cure "battle fatigue" through "excitatory abreaction." Soldiers who suffered from a variety of pathological symptoms (hysterical paralysis, blurred vision, amnesia, etc.) were encouraged to relive the traumatic experiences that caused them, while under the influence of some substance (ether, nitrous oxide) inhibiting their cortical activities and unleashing the emotion.

The researchers quickly realized that for best results the patient had to be put into a highly excited and physically violent state, which would then be followed by a state of exhaustion, general relaxation and calmness, bordering on a loss of consciousness. They also realized that it is not the *quality* of emotion, but its *intensity* that has a therapeutic effect. The violent excitation of the sympathetic division (fight or flight) of the autonomic nervous system often brought a series of "swings" of the autonomic activity (e.g. manifested by alternating laughter and crying), until finally a new balance between excitation and relaxation was achieved. In this way, the entire cortico-hypothalamic relationship was given a jolt, which may have resulted in the weakening of past traumatic "engrams." One of the leading researchers in the field, William Sargant, compares this in his fascinating book, *Battle for the Mind* (1957) with the conditioning that occurs in laboratory dogs when they are subjected to excessive traumatic excitation.

The Russian physiologist Pavlov came to recognize this after an unhappy accident in which his laboratory animals had nearly drowned during a flood in Leningrad in 1924.

They were saved at the last moment, but the powerful emotions of fear and anxiety left an indelible mark on their behaviour. The dogs, which were conditioned to perform various tasks, became "de-conditioned." This happened to various degrees and affected different dogs differently, depending on the "strength" of their temperament. Pavlov differentiated three stages of this "de-conditioning," which is due to traumatic inhibition ("transmarginal inhibition") of the brain centres under the conditions of excessive stress.

In the first stage, a dog would react uniformly to stimuli of different strength. We have parallels to this state in human beings, too, when, under conditions of excessive stress, certain events (such as a death of a relative) which would have ordinarily aroused a powerful emotion, fail to do so. This stage is called "equivalent." In the next stage, called "paradoxical," the reactions would become reversed, with strong stimulus provoking a weak reaction and the other way around. Again, this phenomenon could be observed in human beings. Sargant reports the case of a bomb-shocked patient who could not lower his hand when ordered to do so (strong stimulus) but could do so if he simply thought of reaching for a match in his pocket (weak stimulus). However, the most peculiar reactions occurred when the inhibition reached its most profound "ultra paradoxical" stage, in which an animal's overall conditioning was reversed: it would attack the handler whom it previously liked and become attracted to the one it disliked (Kimble, 1961).

Sargant reports that for positive results to be achieved through excitatory abreaction, the emotional release has to be strong enough to drive the patient into the third final stage of protective inhibition. In one particular case, a battle-shocked soldier could not get rid of the obsessive images of his badly mutilated comrades, which kept popping up in his mind, making him feel very distressed. He was given ether treatment which made him cry, but did not provoke a complete collapse, and so brought no improvement. After the second application of ether, the therapist helped the patient go back to his previous traumatic experiences by urging him on with realistic comments pertaining to the bombing. Finally, the patient began clawing at the couch as if he were back in the ditch, reached a high degree of excitement and collapsed. Upon regaining consciousness, he smiled and said: "Everything has gone. Everything is different. I feel more open, Doctor. I feel better than I did when I came here" (ibid. p. 48).

The frequent application of abreactive treatment associated with a great release of physical and emotional energy is more likely to reverse the patients' former behaviour and also likely to make them, in Sargant's words, "become more suggestible, accepting whatever they are told, however nonsensical, as the inescapable truth." This kind of treatment, if used for a sufficiently extended period of time, is bound to bring some severe physiological repercussions. The repeated shocks to the sympathetic system would gradually "dampen" it and quieten the patient down.[p] This dampening effect would probably account for all the physiological post-Primal changes that Janov reports (lower body temperature, pulse rate, reduced brain wave amplitude and frequency). As Janov writes, the patient's "sex life is less frequent, he does less than he did before, produces less, is less sociable and enjoys being alone more. He also has no great aspirations."

Janov likes to compare the physiology of his "cured" patient to that of a child. This might be true, but only if we think of a child who has been thrashed by his parents and then cried himself/herself into a calming, cathartic, strangely pleasant state of insensitivity and withdrawal.

In some respects, Primal therapy resembles "flooding" techniques used for fear reduction in phobic patients. In flooding, a patient will be exposed for prolonged periods to a situation or an object, causing him to experience his particular fear. This dramatically reduces or even eliminates any fear in future encounters. This technique may work in two ways. Firstly, we are more afraid while anticipating a fearful encounter than when actually undergoing it. Taking the patient right through the entire episode breaks the previous conditioning and reassures him ("I was so scared and yet nothing happened"). The violent fearful reaction, in

---

[p] For a detailed discussion of physiological mechanisms underlying "excitatory abreaction" techniques, see Gellhorn & Loofbourrow (1963, p. 73).

the beginning, could also provoke an opposite swing to calmness once safety is achieved.

Naturally, as with any abreactive technique, some real traumas may be relieved in Primal therapy. The only way for Janov to prove that his therapy produces some unique physiological changes is to have some independent researchers conduct "mock Primals" on hysterically predisposed patients who could repeatedly be thrown (perhaps by hypnotic suggestion) into emotional fits of great intensity. If possible, this "treatment" should be surrounded by some reasonably realistic paraphernalia to enhance the suggestion effect. Janov's attempts to contrast Primals with "mock Primals," in which subjects are merely *pretending* to struggle and scream as if in pain are obviously biasing results of this comparison. It is the severity of the post-Primal emotional collapse and not the purely physical thrashing that matters.

One can only feel compassion for the desperate people who, having paid large sums of money for Primal therapy, find themselves committed to a life of chronic hysteria and the recall of pain. One of Janov's patients who considers himself "cured" (he actually became a Primal therapist himself) tells us that at the beginning of therapy he "was looking for that Godlike eternal bliss and its promise to us in the afterlife: some place where there's no pain and no problems!" Now his answer to the question "Does the Pain end?" is: "Do you ever suppose that someday you will give up eating, or sleeping, or breathing or anything else you do in your life?" In other words, "Pain" has become his life-long companion. The egocentric, attention-craving, relationship-manipulating hysterical fit, which went out of fashion at the beginning of this century, has been made respectable again under the guise of a "Primal." You are insulted by your boss or your husband and, instead of spontaneously "blowing off steam" in some old-fashioned manner, you go off to the bathroom and have a ritualistic "Primal."

After you have been doing this for some years, your emotional "flight or fight" system gets chronically depressed, so that you may, after all, cease to feel pain – without ever having known true joy. (Adobe collection).

Primal therapy has been subjected to such detailed analysis here not because of its popularity which, at any rate, rapidly declined after its heyday in the 70's and 80's, but because it highlights some factors which are relevant to the discussion of other consciousness-modifying techniques.

These factors are:

(1) When people are sufficiently distressed they will clutch literally at any possible solution that comes their way and, given sufficient attention and suitable suggestions, will claim to have greatly benefited from it. This "placebo effect" is being deliberately used even by some respectable specialists and has been successful.

(2) It is a reflection of the psychological climate of our times that a life-denying, pain-oriented philosophy of medieval ghost exorcism has been successfully resurrected, albeit in a pseudo-scientific guise, and is being impressed upon the consciousness of a great number of people.

(3) There is usually an inverse relationship between the intrinsic value of any consciousness-modifying approach and the amount of mystifying paraphernalia, neologisms and Messianic ballyhoo that accompanies it. More often than not, the intrinsically valuable part has already been known for hundreds and sometimes thousands of years. Most attempts to present some "radically new approach" to the human psychology appear to be based either on ignorance or on conscious intention to deceive.

The *Janov Primal Center* still operates in Santa Monica, CA.

IV. Hare Krishna

It is convenient to look at the Hare Krishna phenomenon after discussing Primal therapy, for similarities and dissimilarities between these two approaches tend to highlight each other. For those not familiar with the Hare Krishna movement, it may be briefly described as a modern offshoot of the Krishna worship cult, based on the chanting of "Maha Mantra" ("The Great Mantra": Hare Krishna Hare Krishna Krishna Krishna Hare Hare Hare Rama Hare Rama Rama Rama Hare Hare). It follows an elaborate system of devotion to and belief in various supernatural personalities, whose putative biographical data are provided in exhaustive detail by the main exponent of the movement Swami A. C. Bhaktivedanta Prabhupada (1993).

It is heartening indeed to shift our weary attention from the pain and pessimism of Primal philosophy to the almost pagan joyousness of the Krishna devotees. In one of his numerous expositions of Yoga philosophy, Prabhupada explicitly states that not only all human endeavours but also all Yogic efforts are undertaken in search of happiness. A Yogi, instead of choosing the transient joys of life, looks for lasting sense gratification in "Ananta" – Union with the Supreme. But, gratification it remains.

Recognizing the role of pleasure, Prabhupada nonetheless denies that meditation is the way to achieve the Ultimate Bliss. He regards it as being inappropriate for this Age. There is a paradox here: how is it possible to advocate Bliss-consciousness without the "Supreme peace" which, as we have surmised, can be gained through meditation? If we look closely at the symptoms of the ecstatic experiences that Prabhupada describes, we may be able to resolve this paradox.

These symptoms are:

1) Dancing;
2) Rolling on the ground;
3) Singing loudly;
4) Stretching the body;
5) Crying loudly;
6) Yawning;
7) Breathing heavily;
8) Neglecting the presence of others;
9) Drooling;
10) Laughing like a madman;
11) Wheeling of the head;
12) Belching

Sometimes experiences of "ecstatic love for Krishna" may also be accompanied by "trembling of the whole body and haemorrhaging from some part of the body." "Ancillary" ecstatic symptoms are:

1) Becoming stunned;
2) Perspiration;
3) Standing of hairs on the body;
4) Faltering of the voice;
5) Trembling;
6) Changing of bodily colour;
7) Tears; and, finally
8) Devastation

Hare Krishna. (Adobe collection).

These symptoms would presumably be induced by prolonged and repeated chanting of the Hare Krishna Mantra, possibly in an atmosphere of an emotion-charged devotional gathering. The similarity between these symptoms and those provoked at Revivalist meetings is undeniable. The Revival meetings held by Jonathan Edwards in America, John Wesley in England, and Evan Roberts in Wales were accompanied by crying, screaming, speaking in tongues, dancing, epileptic movements and cataleptic states. There is a fairly general agreement among students of this phenomenon that these and other features of Revival meetings (such as the notorious "barkers" and "jumpers") are manifestations of group hysteria. This, however, was a belated recognition. At the time the various bizarre manifestations of group hysteria, even those that led people to behave like animals, were regarded to be a sure sign of Heavenly favour. As one observer noted:

> When attacked by the jerks, the victims of enthusiasm sometimes leapt like frogs and exhibited every grotesque and hideous contortion of the face and limbs. The barks consisted of getting down on all fours, growling, snapping the teeth, and barking like dogs... These last (who barked like dogs) were particularly gifted in prophesies, trances, dreams, rhapsodies, visions of angels, of heaven, and of the holy city.

Even the New World was not spared the contagion, with hysterical symptoms resembling those that prevailed in the British Isles:

> ...trembling, weeping and swooning away, till every appearance of life was gone, and the extremities of the body assumed the coldness of a corpse. At one meeting, not less than a thousand persons fell to the ground apparently without sense or motion.

The particular symptoms chosen would depend on the "leaders." The great suggestibility of hysterics and their tendency to imitate others has already been pointed out. The seemingly uncontrollable behaviour (as in "Primals") actually shows great susceptibility to being shaped by example and expectations. As has been found in cases of hysterical contagion, a single person may inspire an outbreak in a large and suitably prepared crowd. The epidemics of hysteria have not been a prerogative of the Middle Ages. We find reports of some outbreaks in Tanzania and East Africa in 1962 and 1964. In each case, hundreds of individuals were involved. Adolescents, being more suggestible and imitation-prone, are found to be particularly susceptible to hysterical contagion.

Still, it would be an over-simplification to say that all the effects of Hare Krishna chanting are limited to the influence of hysterical contagion. It is entirely possible for individuals to be triggered into contact with some of the subconscious centres through repeated chanting of a rhythmic mantra. The occasional cross-talk, particularly if it involves the pleasure areas, would have to be of a transient nature, because physical activity (dancing, etc.) prevents prolonged maintenance of this fragile state.

In chanting, as well as in "Primaling," there will be a certain swing to calm parasympathetic activity *after the chanting is stopped*. Which technique is more efficient in this respect? This is hard to say. "Primaling" has greater intensity of emotion on its side. Chanting, though usually gentler, incorporates rhythmic stimulation, which may hit just the right frequency and lead to a more direct activation of the emotional centres in the brain. It would be interesting to compare the physiological effects of prolonged chanting with those of "Primaling." The Hare Krishna devotees may also justifiably lay claim to greater naturalness of their method. They do not need the strobe light to trigger their hair-raising experiences. Their suggested repertoire is more diverse and gives more scope to the individual imagination. Their sense of devotion (if real) can certainly give them an illusion of "cosmic unity" that the Maharishi tried to reserve only for meditators who sometimes spent tens of thousands of dollars on "advanced techniques."

Overall, barring the inevitable Messianic and sectarian overtones, the Hare Krishna movement seems to be suitable for people who need a drastic change in their lifestyle and are naturally attracted to the more dramatic aspects of a religious group experience. After years of chanting they may look forward to greater calmness and if they are suitably endowed, even some transient "transcendental bliss."

They can also become great vegetarian cooks, a definite plus for the society!

Epilogue

"Man is an epidemic, multiplying at a superexponential rate, destroying the environment upon which he depends, and threatening his extinction. He treats the world as a storehouse existing for his delectation; he plunders, rapes, poisons, and kills this living system, the biosphere, in ignorance of its workings and its fundamental value...Survival of man is contingent upon categorical rejection of this cultural inferiority complex that is the Western view and its replacement with the ecological view – a man in nature. This reveals the ways of the working world and shows our ignorant interventions as self-mutilation, leading to suicide, genocide, biocide."

Ian L. McHarg
The 1971 B.Y. Morrison Memorial Lecture
US Agricultural Research Service

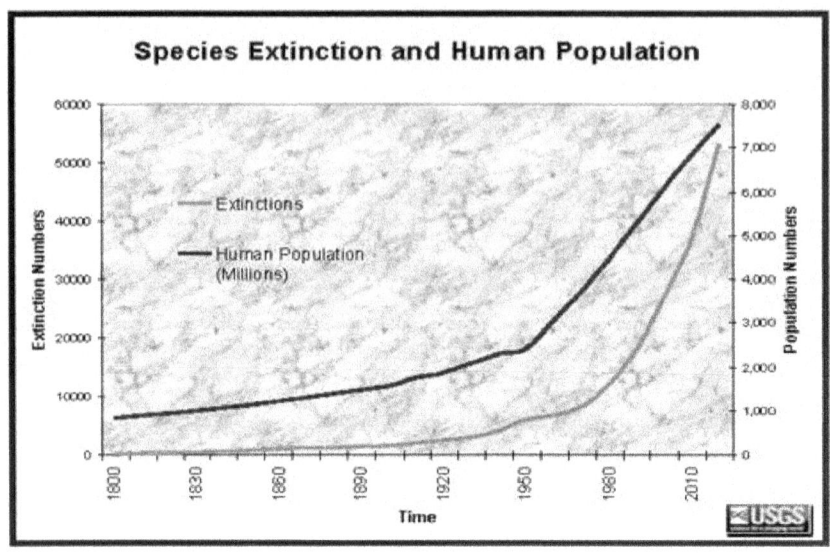

Half of all marine life lost **in just 40 years.** (Viegas, 2015)

Ian L. McHarg (1920-2001), was a blunt Scottish-born scientist and horticulturist who gave us many ornamental plants to make our lives more beautiful. He, together with Loren Eiseley, another man with a global and unblinkered vision of the world saw man as essentially a form of planetary disease, a plant parasite on a suicidal binge, a locust that developed not only the internal combustion engine to aid its flight, but a nuclear bomb to end all life on earth.

Man, the ever-restless post-arboreal primate, whose perilous journey began as a tiny but ambitious rodent, repressed for too long by the stampeding and carnivorous dinosaurs, did what every animal had to do, which is to survive at all costs; but then, having survived, decided that he would never again let nature catch him with his pants down. So, he created an artificial world in which he tried to re-manufacture his arboreal paradise, with easy access to food, shelter and mates, whom he finds now not through mating calls and smells but through smartphone apps. He claims to have transcended nature, but remains a short-sighted, poorly toilet trained (look at all the pollution from domestic sources, let alone industrial activity!), status-seeking, sex-crazy, Twitter-obsessed, occasionally co-operative but mostly selfish, xenophobic creature; a chattering terrestrial primate, justifying his bad habits by any form of ideology or religion that his overgrown brain will conjure up.

He seemed to be engaged in some phenotypic "repetition compulsion" by recreating, through his construction of a consumer "paradise," the dry, hot and barren savannah from which he once barely escaped with his life. His millenarian and cultish attempts to recapture the lost paradise, at least in his head, through the various religions and spiritual tricks have had not one iota of effect on his earthly predicament.

Calls of alarm have sounded in recent times by prominent thinkers such as Jared Diamond, E.O. Wilson, and others, calling for some reconciliation between man and nature, and man's insatiable desires multiplied by his growing numbers. Since the Industrial Revolution, our ranks have swelled from one billion to seven billion, a rate of growth that biologist E.O. Wilson has characterized as "more bacterial than primate." If you put the mass of all the humans together, they will weigh more than any other large species on Earth combined. Human greed and human numbers (and human ingenuity) have combined to produce the Great Acceleration of the Anthropocene – the Age of unprecedented exploitation of the biosphere by man. E.O. Wilson even sounded a call to religious leaders to forget differences between science and religion and try to save what is left of the Creation. Alas, his calls have fallen on deaf ears. Another prophetic voice, that of James Lovelock (2000), the originator of the Gaia concept, has also grown a bit hoarse, calling now to accept such desperate measures as hydraulic fracturing to keep at least our streetlights and our iPads working, without which our civilization, he fears, would descend into chaos.

However, it is not thinkers or intellectuals who seem to have at least a marginal effect on human affairs, but high-status individuals whose wealth and power elevate them above the petty desires for self-promotion, self-aggrandizement and self-enrichment that our politicians and other "opinion leaders" are suffering from. In July 2012 world leaders, spurred on by the Bill and Melinda Gates Foundation, gathered in London to address the long-buried issue of birth control. Bill and Melinda Gates address this issue by talking about the need to save women's lives and to promote health and future well-being of their children. They know it may be too little and too late to ameliorate the worst abuses of the divine dictum "Be fruitful and multiply," but they feel that they may at least alleviate the suffering of millions of women in poor countries who die in childbirth or produce offspring that have no chance of a happy and healthy life.

Alas, there is no long-term technological fix to humanity's problems. Condoms, for which the Australian government annually spends large sums of money, trying to curtail the spread of AIDS in Papua New Guinea, are used mainly as improvised fish lures by the crafty natives, whose beauty-conscious wives are using condom lubricants as hair and face cosmetics.

In Aldous Huxley's vision of the *Brave New World*, people were genetically pre-conditioned and controlled through their predilection for pleasure and comfort. In Orwell's

1984, the subjects were cowed by an all-pervasive fear of surveillance. In Stanislaw Lem's *The Futurological Congress*, an ephemeral, drug-induced world transformed reality into a hedonistic but fake *Brave New World*. In every case, starting with H. G. Wells and the Zamyatin's *We*, the world population was split into manipulators and manipulated.

Which vision is closer to reality? All of them are. There are people right now who co-exist in such utopian and anti-utopian worlds. Where does the sub-Saharan Africa or Belarus fit in? Will it ever be so, even as we continue to squander our planet's resources and its biodiversity, with the haves and the have-nots co-existing in slums and gated communities, poles or almost worlds apart? There should be little doubt in the reader's mind that, given the failures of our recent past, any attempts to burp, convulse, mediate, pray, and otherwise lead or inspire people into some high-minded reality is in itself a utopian and absurd notion.

Yet, despite all that has been said, I do want to leave the reader with a dream.

It is fashionable now to talk about Big History, which is a way of looking at things in largely historical perspective, sometimes harkening all the way to Big Bang. Let us indulge at least in a Medium-Big History exercise by going back to that humble but ambitious rodent, the post-Jurassic predecessor of all mammals, coming out of its hiding into the light of the oxygen-rich and verdant world.

You see, it was a little psychic rodent. It had a premonition of what is going to happen to its far-off offspring who will forget about their humble origins and their dependence on plants and oxygen and water and will pollute their nests with deadly chemicals and radioactive debris. They will then try all sorts of half-measures and will hold innumerable conferences to determine a solution to their self-inflicted dilemma.

A little psychic rodent. (Adobe collection).

The rodent sits back on its haunches and sniffs the air, wrinkling its nose at me, sounding an alarm call. It proceeds to tell me that, if these distant offspring are to survive, they will need to evolve differently – simultaneously backwards and forwards. They will have to go back all the way to a photosynthesizing and yet thinking human/plant hybrid to save themselves and the planet they inhabit. Their ecological footprint will need to shrink to the size of their physical feet – or less. They will need to stop poisoning plants and killing animals, including themselves. Then, eventually, with enough pointed backwards evolution, they will recall, Buddha-like, all their evolutionary steps. They will feel, with every cell of their bodies, their connection to the cosmos and to what they used to call "God." Through genetic manipulation that will then become routine, they may then choose another physical incarnation, more in tune with their newly acquired wisdom. That will be their true accomplishment and grandeur, a true *"religere,"* a reconnection, anticipated by seers throughout ages.

This was all foretold by a small, prehistoric rodent, a being who held in his tiny skull the link between man and dinosaur. It is a good, true story, half of which has already materialized and can be read on the stone pages of the fossil record, but much of the writing that must now be done can only be set down in far more ephemeral type. We, the offspring, beings who literally "sprung" into our intelligence and who are constantly having our mental traps "sprung" upon us, must learn new kinds of living if we are to heed the rodent's warning. We must re-master the wiring of the mind, with all its hastily constructed synapses and the inevitable evolutionary typos. We must push harder to decipher the multi-layered Rosetta Stone of the human brain so that we may translate the universal message of so many religions and philosophies into a commonly understood human vernacular. Finally, we must learn to inscribe ourselves more conscientiously and sustainably on the pages of our small chapter of the universe, leaving room and hope for other authors to come after us.

And so the world may begin again,
And so the world may begin again…
Not with a Bang but with a promise…

About the extraordinary life of Pyotr Patrushev

Sydney Morning Herald, 30th of April, 2016

In 1962, Pyotr Patrushev, a Siberian village boy, swimming champion of the Soviet era, persecuted army conscript and then an inmate of a notorious psychiatric prison/hospital, became the sole survivor of swimming from Batumi, a Black Sea coastal resort near the Turkish border, to freedom (and prison) in Turkey.

He gained refugee status and worked as a journalist for the BBC in London, and later hosted two radio shows for Radio Liberty in Munich and San Francisco, broadcasting cultural/scientific programs to the USSR during the Cold War. He eventually settled in Australia and created a remarkably successful interpreting and translation practice. He interpreted for the ABC, SBS and Prime Ministers Kevin Rudd and John Howard when they met Mikhail Gorbachev, Vladimir Putin and other heads of state.

Pyotr Patrushev was born in Kolpashevo, a Siberian village on May 26, 1942. His father, Egor Grigorievich

Patrushev, was a vet who died fighting in World War II a month before Pyotr was born. Pyotr's mother was Marina Vasilievna Leschina, who brought up three kids without a husband after the war.

Patrushev was training at a college in Tomsk and was a competitive swimmer, a champion in the backstroke, he participated in competitions in Moscow and around the country, which gave him prestige and food coupons, and in the early 60s was training for the Tokyo Olympic Games.

After graduating from college, Patrushev was trying to get into university but was summoned to join the army. He was supposed to be an elite athlete in the sports club of the Soviet Army in Novosibirsk – a factory of future champions.

But he did not know then, and only learned the details 50 years later, that he was caught up in the middle of political intrigue.

He and his swimming trainer, Henry Bulakin, were apparently hated by the director of the Tomsk swimming centre, a man named Shkolnik, a former associate of Stalin's brutal security chief Lavrentiy Beria, who was exiled to Siberia after Beria's execution. Just one phone call from him to Novosibirsk's KGB decided Patrushev's fate.

Suddenly from the Athletic Club, he was transferred to a regular military unit. Although he had been snatched by the army before he could take up tertiary education, his mid-teens discovery of English literature at the college in Tomsk set him on the path of escape from the USSR.

Having repeatedly been threatened during his time in the army and in fear of his life, Patrushev decided to resort to tricks and passed himself off as a mental patient.

By bizarre behaviour he got himself sent to the Tomsk psychiatric hospital where he faked a mental illness – no small feat. He applied an in-depth grasp of medicine and the crucial Soviet distinction between psychiatric "malingering" and "treatments".

When he learnt from his medical student friends that the psychopathic doctor was going to use gruesome torture drug "treatments" he made a daring escape from the high-security psychiatric facility dressed in his mental patient's pyjamas. He stayed at his trainer's place for a couple of days, and as a result, his trainer and his whole family suffered and were to be persecuted all their lives.

His experience as a conscript, and in the psychiatric hospital, made the escape a matter of necessity to save his life. This prompted Patrushev's journey to the Black Sea region, and his eventual swim to Turkey. He set out south from Tomsk, with no proper clothes or documentation, the only shelter given on the way by his swimming coach. (Later he felt deeply responsible for the persecution that befell his coach, and for years did his best to help him and his family with financial and moral support).

The swim from Batumi was unique – no other Russian refugee would survive the Black Sea swim to Turkey. It wasn't only the strong currents or the freezing upsurges of water that were worrying. It was dodging nets, searchlights, surveillance planes, submarines, sonar, radar, depth charges and patrol boats.

On arrival in Turkey, he was jailed as a Soviet spy, was regularly interrogated and sent more than once before a firing squad to be shot with fake bullets. Patrushev was condemned to death in absentia by the Soviet authorities and was on the KGB's wanted list for over 25 years.

Pyotr Patrushev's extraordinary life and work have been well documented by friends and admirers, most accessible in four short YouTube videos, *The Man who Swam from Russia*, by filmmaker Mike Rubbo – as well as ABC interviews with Richard Fidler, Robyn Williams and Caroline Jones.

"The life of Russian translator and interpreter Pyotr Patrushev is the stuff adventure stories are made of. Pyotr is a fascinating, extraordinary man, a great Australian," said Fidler.

Patrushev frequently wrote for Australian newspapers, radio and television. He worked in the nineties as a senior consultant in the former USSR for Stella and Helen Cornelius' Conflict Resolution Network (CRN), a pillar of the Centre for Peace and Conflict Studies at Sydney University. In Moscow, he established a CRN for Russia and published his own translation of the CRN's *Everyone Can Win* (Cornelius & Faire, 1998).

Pyotr Patrushev died after a stroke at Murrays beach in his beloved Jervis Bay on March 28. He is survived by wife Alice Messerer, son Andrei and daughter Reema from his previous marriage.

He had suffered poor health in recent years, primarily attributable to the impact of his brutal and traumatic early life in Russia. His death is a monumental loss: his lively mind and engaging personality will be deeply missed by his many friends.

Pyotr Patrushev's website: www.pyotr-patrushev.com

Peter King, Sydney University, 2016

References

Adobe (2016). [images]. Reprinted with kind permission of Adobe stock premium collection. [© Adobe Systems Incorporated.]

Alacoque, St. M. M. (1986). *The autobiography of St. Margaret Mary Alacoque*. Rockford, IL: Tan Books.

Aphrodisias, A. of. (2012). *On the soul. Part I: Soul as form of the body, parts of the soul, nourishment, and perception*. London, Great Britain: Bristol Classical Press.

Annau, Z., Heffner, R., & Koob, G. F. (1974, August). Electrical self-stimulation of single and multiple loci: long term observations. *Physiology & Behavior, 13*(2), 281-290.

Aretaeus, of Cappadocia. (2010). *Aretæus, consisting of eight books, on the causes, symptoms and cure of acute and chronic diseases* [translated from the original Greek]. (John Moffat, M.D. trans). Farmington Hills, MI: Gale ECCO, Print Editions.

Arnold, M. B. (1960). *Emotion and personality*. (Vol 2.) New York, NY: Columbia.

Augustine, St. (2012). *The confessions of St. Augustine*. [Dayboro]: Emereo Pub. (n.p.).

Avila, T. (2005, July). Teresa of Ávila: The interior castle. *Theology Today, 62*(2), 230-234.

Avila, S. T. (2013). *The way of perfection*. CreateSpace Independent Publishing Platform.

Banquet, J. P. (1973, August). Spectral analysis of the EEG in meditation. *Electroencephalography and Clinical Neurophysiology, 35*.

Baudouin, C. (2016). (Paul, E & Paul, C. trans.) *Suggestion and autosuggestion: A psychological and pedagogical study based upon the investigations made by the New Nancy School*. South Yarra, Victoria: Leopold Classic Library.

Bean, W.B. (1962). Brain memory and learning - a neurologist's view. *Archives of Internal Medicine. 110*(6), 913-914. doi:10.1001/archinte.1962.03620240095018

Bernheim, H. (1993). *Hypnosis & suggestion in psychotherapy by H. Bernheim*. New York, NY: Jason Aronson, Inc.

Big History Project. (2016). Retrieved from https://school.bighistoryproject.com/

Bishop, M.P., Elder S.T, Heath R.G. (1963, April). Intracranial self-stimulation in man. *Science, 140*(3565), 394-6.

Bourne, P.G. (2013). *Acute drug abuse emergencies: A treatment manual*. New York, NY: Elsevier.

Bowers, M.B. Jr. & Friedman, D.X. (1966, September). Psychedelic experiences in acute psychoses. *Archives of General Psychiatry, 15*, 240-248.

Brace, C.L., (1964). The fate of the 'classic' Neanderthals: A consideration of Hominid catastrophism, *Current Anthropology, 5*, 3-43

Breakey, W. R (1974). Hallucinogenic drugs as precipitants of schizophrenia. *Psychological Medicine*, 4: 255-261.

Breuer, J. & Freud, S. (2000). *Studies on hysteria* (Reiss. ed.). New York, NY: Basic Books.

Broome, M.R., Woolley, J.B., Tabraham, P., Johns, L.C., Bramon, E., Murray, G.K., Pariante, C., McGuire P.K., Murray, R.M. (2005, November). What causes the onset of psychosis? *Schizophrenia Research.* 79, 23–34

Burkitt, I. & Sullivan, P. (2009, September). Embodied ideas and divided selves: Revisiting Laing via Bakhtin. *British Journal of Social Psychology, 48*, 563–577.

Bushak, L. (2015, September). *Medical Daily: doctors might soon prescribe LSD for anxiety*. Retrieved from: http://www.medicaldaily.com/anxiety-and-mental-health-psychedelic-drugs-may-be-latest-treatment-range-disorders-351650

Cannon, W.B. (1957, May). Voodoo death. *Psychosomatic Medicine, 19*(3), 182–190.

Chance, M.R.A. (1963). A Biological Perspective on Convulsions. *Colloques Internationaux du Centre National de la Recherche Scientifique. 12.* Paris: Seuil.

Chance, M.R.A. (1984). Biological systems synthesis of mentality and the nature of the two modes of mental operation: Hedonic and agonic. *Man-Environment Systems, 14*, 143-157

Chen, W., Liu, J., Zhang, L., Xu, H., Guo, X., Deng, S., Li, Z. (2014, June). Generation of the SCN1A epilepsy mutation in hiPS cells using the TALEN technique. *Scientific reports, 4* (5404).

Cleary, T. (1998). *The Sutra of Hui-Neng: Grand Master of Zen* (1st ed.). Boston MA: Shambhala.

Climacus, St. J. (1978). *The Ladder of Divine Ascent.* Boston, MA: Holy Transfiguration Monastery.

Cohen, S. (1967). *The beyond within: The LSD story.* New York, NY: Atheneum.

Cole, M. (2007). Book reviews - the autobiography of Alexander Luria: A dialogue with the making of mind. *The American Journal of Psychology, 120*(1), 153.

Conze, E. (Trans.). (1959). *Buddhist Scriptures.* Harmondsworth, Great Britain: Penguin.

Cornelius, H., & Faire, S. (1998). *Everyone Can Win: How to Resolve Conflict.* Pymble, NSW, Australia. London, Great Britain: Simon & Schuster Australia.

Cross, St. (2015). *The ascent of mount Carmel.* CreateSpace Independent Publishing Platform.

Crow, J.F. (1966). The quality of people: Human evolutionary changes. *Bioscience, 16,* 863-7

Crowley, A. (2014). *Magick*. CreateSpace Independent Publishing Platform.

Cusa, N. of. (2005). Nicholas of Cusa: selected spiritual writings. (H. L. Bond, Trans.) (1st pap. ed.). Mahwah, NJ: Paulist Press.

Debenham, G.. Hill D., Sargant, W., Slater E. (1941). Treatment of war neurosis. *The Lancet, 237*(6126), 107-109. doi:10.1016/S0140-6736(00)77449-6

Delgado, J.M.R. (1971). *Physical control of the mind - toward a psychocivilized society* (2nd ed.). New York, NY: Harper & Row.

Pirijano, A.D. (1955). *A Cure for Serpents: A Doctor in Africa.* London: Andre Deutsche.

DeVore, I. (1965). *Primate behavior.* New York, NY: Holt, Rinehart and Winston.

Dewhurst, K., & Beard, A. (1970). Sudden religious conversions in temporal lobe epilepsy. *The British Journal of Psychiatry: The Journal of Mental Science, 117*(540), 497–507.

Dostoyevsky F. M. in Memoirs of his Contemporaries. (1923). Fedor Mikhaylovich Dostoyevskiy v vospominaniyakh sovremennikov i v yego pis'makh. Vtoroye ispravlennoye i dopolnennoye izdaniye [Dostoevsky's biography in documents and memoirs of his contemporaries]. (2nd rev. ed.). Moscow, Russia: Moskva. Izdatel'stvo.

Dostoevsky, F. & Dalton, E. (2004). *The Possessed* (Garnett, C., trans.; Engl. lang. ed.). New York, NY: Barnes & Noble Classics.

Dostoyevsky, F. (2016). *The Idiot.* Csorna, Hungary: Sheba Blake Publishing.

Easwaran, E. (2007). *The Dhammapada* (2nd ed.). Tomales, CA: Nilgiri Press.

Eknath, E. & Nagler, M.N. (2007). *The Upanishads* (2nd ed.). Tomales, CA: Nilgiri Press.

Ernst, G. (2010). *Tommaso Campanella: the book and the body of nature.* Dordrecht, NY: Springer.

Fedorchek, R. M. (2007). Treatise on love of God. *Choice: Current Reviews For Academic Libraries, 44*(12), 2124

Fiantesev, S. (2017a). *Primate.* Reprinted with kind permission of the artist.

Fiantesev, S. (2017b). *What's it all about.* Reprinted with kind permission of the artist.

Fiantesev, S. (2017c). *A feeling of bliss.* Reprinted with kind permission of the artist.

Fiantesev, S. (2017d). *Look into the fire.* Reprinted with kind permission of the artist.

Fiantesev, S. (2017e). *The sound of one hand clapping.* Reprinted with kind permission of the artist.

Fiantesev, S. (2017f). *Love and reverence.* Reprinted with kind permission of the artist.

Fiantesev, S. (2017g). *Primal scream.* Reprinted with kind permission of the artist.

Fletcher, R. (2007, June). Understanding marijuana, a new look at the scientific evidence by Mitch Earleywine. *Occupational Medicine, 57*(2), 157-158.

French, R.K. (1969). *Robert Whytt, the soul, and medicine.* London, Great Britain: Wellcome Institute of the History of Medicine.

Freud, S. (1909). Notes upon a case of obsessional neurosis. *Standard edition, 10*(151), 320.

Gallacher, P. (1997). *The cloud of unknowing*. Kalamazoo, MI: Medieval Institute Publications.

Gellhorn, E. & G. N. Loofbourrow, G. N. (1963). *Emotions & emotional disorders; a neurophysiological study*. New York, NY: Hoeber Medical Division.

Gopi, K. (1997). *Kundalini: The evolutionary energy in man* (rev. ed.). Boston, MA & New York, NY: Shambhala.

Greeley, A.M. (1974). *Ecstasy: A way of knowing*. Englewood Cliffs, N.J.: Prentice-Hall.

Green, J.D. (1964, October). The Hippocampus. *Physiological Reviews, 44* (4), 561–608.

Greenberg, J.H. (1959, October). Current trends in linguistics. *Science. 130,* (3383), 1165-70

Goodall, J. (1999). *In the shadow of man*. London, Great Britain: Phoenix.

Happold, F.C. (1970). *Mysticism: a study and an anthology* (rev. ed.). Harmondsworth, United Kingdom: Penguin Books.

Herbert, M.D. Spiegel. (2004). *Trance and Treatment Clinical Uses of Hypnosis Paperback* (2nd ed.). American Psychiatric Publishing, Inc. Retrieved from http://trove.nla.gov.au/version/208154530

Heath R.G. (1964). *The Role of Pleasure in Behavior*. New York, NY: Harper & Row

Heath, R.G.; Mickle, W.A. (2013). *Evaluation of seven years' experience with depth electrode studies in human patients. Electrical Studies on the Unanesthetized Brain*. New York, NY: PB Hoeber.

Hippocrates. (1923). *Hippocrates, Volume II: Prognostic*. (W. H. S. Jones, Trans.). Cambridge, Mass.: Harvard University Press.

Hughes, J. (1994, July). Post-traumatic stress disorder: An evaluation of behavioural and cognitive behavioural interventions and treatments. *Clinical Psychology & Psychotherapy, 1*(3), 125-142. doi:10.1002/cpp.5640010301

Humphreys, C. (1998). *Concentration and meditation: A manual of mind development* (4th ed.). Boston, MA: Element Books Ltd.

Huxley, A. (2009). *The perennial philosophy* (1st Harper Perennial Modern classics ed.). New York, NY: Harper Perennial Modern Classics.

Huxley, A. (2013). *Brave new world* (Reprint ed.). New York, NY: Everyman's Library.

Huxley, A. (2009). *The doors of perception and heaven and hell*. New York, NY: Harper Perennial Modern Classics.

Ilf, I., & Petrov, E. (1997). The twelve chairs (Tran. ed.). Evanston, IL: Northwestern University Press.

Inagaki, T.K., & Eisenberger, N. I. (2012, January). Neural correlates of giving support to a loved one. *Psychosomatic Medicine, 74*(1), 3-7.

James, W. (1971). *The varieties of religious experience*. London, England: Collins

James, W. & Abzug, R. (2013). *The varieties of religious experience*. Boston, MA: Bedford/St. Martins.

Janov, A. (1971). *The anatomy of mental illness the scientific bases of Primal therapy*. New York, NY: G. P. Putnams's Sons.

Janov, A. (1972). *Primal revolution*. New York, NY: Simon & Schuster.

Janov, A., & Holden, E. M. (1975). Primal Man: The New Consciousness (1st ed.). New York: Crowell.

Jerison, H.J. (1973). *Evolution of the brain and intelligence*. New York, NY: Academic Press.

Jersild, A.T. & Holmes, F.B. (1935). Children's fears. *Child Development Monographs,* 20. ix-358

Jerome, J. K. (2015). *Three Men in a Boat.* CreateSpace Independent Publishing Platform

Johnson, W. J. (Trans.). (2009). *The Bhagavad Gita* (rev. ed.). Oxford, Great Britain: Oxford University Press.

Karlsson, S.G. & Larsson, K. (1975). Self-stimulation and mating behavior in the male rat. *Scandinavian Journal of Psychology, 16*(1), 7–10.

Kiev, A. (1972). *Transcultural psychiatry.* New York, NY: Free Press.

Killam, E.K., Killam, & K.F, Shaw T. (1957). The effects of psychotherapeutic compounds on central afferent and limbic pathways. *The Annals of the New York Academy of Sciences, 66*(3), 784-805.

Kimble, G. A. (1961). *Hilgard and Marquis' Conditioning and Learning.* New York: Appleton-Century-Crofts

Klee, B. (1963, May). Lysergic acid diethylamide (LSD-25) and ego functions. *Archives of General Psychiatry, 8*(5), 461-474.

Knox, R.A. (2000). *Enthusiasm: A Chapter in the history of religion with special reference to the 17th and 18th centuries.* New York, NY: Oxford University Press.

Koestler, A. (2011). *Arrow in the blue* (new ed.). Vintage Digital.

Koestler, A. (1990). *The ghost in the machine.* London, Great Britain: Penguin (Non-Classics).

Kotsopoulos, S. (1986). Aretaeus the Cappadocian on mental illness. *Comprehensive Psychiatry, 27*(2), 171-179.

Kotsonis, I. (1997). An Athonite Gerontikon: Sayings of the Holy Fathers of Mount Athos. Thessaloniki, Greece: Publications of the Holy Monastery of St. Gregory Palamas.

Krishnamurti J. (1972). (photograph by Mary Zimbalist (© the Estate of Mary Zimbalist). Reprinted with kind permission of the copyright holder.

Krishnamurti, J.K. (2001). *You are the world: authentic reports of talks and discussions in American universities.* Chennai, India: Krishnamurti Foundation India.

Krishnamurti, J.K. (1969). *The First and last Freedom.* London, England: Victor Gollancz

Krishnamurti, J.K. (2013). *The first and last freedom.* London, Great Britain: Rider & Co.

Krishnamurti, J.K. (1973). *The Awakening of the Intelligence.* London, Great Britain: Victor Gollancz

Kulvalayananda, S. (2014). *Gheranda Samhita.* Maharashtra, India: Kaivalyadhama Samiti Lonavla

La Barre, W.L. (2010). *The ghost dance: The origins of religion* (2nd rev. ed.). Kent, Great Britain: Crescent Moon Publishing.

Laing, R.D. (1967). *The politics of experience and the bird of paradise.* London, Great Britain: Harmondsworth Penguin.

Lautch, H. (1971). Dental phobia. *British Journal of Psychiatry, 119,* 151–158.

Lazarus R., Opton. E.M., Nomikos, M.S., Rankin, N.O. (1965). The principle of short-circuiting of threat: Further evidence. *Journal of Personality, 33*(4), 622-35.

Lazarus, R.S. (2006). Emotions and interpersonal relationships: toward a person-centered conceptualization of emotions and coping. *Journal of Personality, 74,* 9-46.

Laski, M. (1961). *Ecstasy: a study of some secular and religious experiences.* London, Great Britain: The Cresset Press.

Leakey, R.E. (1973, June). Skull 1470. *National Geographic,* 819-29.

Leboyer, F. (1975). *Birth without violence by Frederick Leboyer.* New York, NY: Alfred Knopf

Ludwig, A., Levine J., Stark L., Lazar R. (1969, July). A clinical study of LSD treatment in alcoholism. *Am J Psychiatry, 126* (1), 59–69.

Luria, A. R. *The Mind of the Mnemonist*. London, Great Britain: Jonathan Cape, 1968.

Lilly, J.C. (1958). Learning motivated by subcortical stimulation: The 'start' and 'stop' patterns of behavior. *In The Reticular Formation of the Brain.* H. H. Jasper, et al. (Eds.) Boston, MA: Little Brown & Co.

Lishman, W. (1974). The speed of recall of pleasant and unpleasant experiences. *Psychological Medicine*, 4(2), 212-218.

Livingston, R.B. (1967). *Reinforcement. The Neurosciences: a study program.* New York, NY: Rockefeller University Press.

Lombroso, C. (1891). The man of genius. New York, NY: C. Scribner's sons.

Lombroso, C. (2016). *The man of genius* (Ann. 2nd ed.). London, United Kingdom: Wermod and Wermod Publishing Group.

Lord, B. (2010). *Saint Catherine de Ricci*. Manila, Philippines: Journeys of Faith.

Lovelock, J. (2000). *Gaia: The Practical Science of Planetary Medicine.* (2nd ed.). London, United Kingdom: Gaia Books Ltd.

MacDonald, M. (ed.). (2013). *Witchcraft and Hysteria in Elizabethan London: Edward Jorden and the Mary Glover Case* (rep. ed.). Abingdon, United Kingdom: Routledge.

MacLean, P.D. (1990). *The triune brain in evolution: Role in paleocerebral functions.* New York, NY: Springer.

MacLean, P.D. (1952, November). Some psychiatric implications of physiological studies on frontotemporal portions of limbic system (visceral brain). *Electroencephalography and Clinical Neurophysiology*, 4 (4), 407-418.

MacLean, P.D. (1971). *The triune brain, emotion, and scientific bias.* The Neurosciences, Second Study Program, Francis O.

Schmitt (Editor-in-Chief). New York, NY: The Rockefeller University Press.

MacLean, P.D. (1973). *A triune concept of the brain and behavior*. Toronto and Buffalo, CA: University of Toronto Press.

Maharishi M.Y. (1969). *On the Bhagavad Gita, a new translation and commentary*. Harmondsworth, Great Britain: Penguin

Maharishi M.Y. (1968). *The science of being and the art of living: Transcendental meditation*. New York, NY: New American Library.

Maharishi M. H. (photograph by Bahgavan, © Sri Ramanasramam). Reprinted with kind permission of the copyright holder. Retrieved from http://www.sriramanamaharshi.org/portfolio-item/bhagavan-color-photo-gallery/

Magnus,O., de Haas, A.M.L., Vinken, P.J., Bruyn, G.W. (Eds.). (1974). *Handbook of Clinical Neurology: The Epilepsies*. Amsterdam, Netherlands: North-Holland Publishing.*15*; 295–301.

Malmo, R. (1961). Slowing of heart-rate after septal self-stimulation in tats. *Science, 133*, 1128-30.

MAPS - Research. (2016). Retrieved from http://www.maps.org/research/

Marais, E. *The soul of the ape*. London, United Kingdom: Penguin, 1973.

Mathews, A. M. (1971). Physiological approaches to the investigation of desensitization. *Psychology Bulletin, 76*, 73-83.

Mead, G.R.S. (2010). *Mundakopanishad*. Whitefish, MO: Kessinger Publishing, LLC.

Merlis, J. K. (1974). Reflex epilepsy. *Handbook of clinical neurology, 15*, 449.

McGlothlin, W., Cohen, S., & McGlothlin M.S. (1967, November). Long lasting effects of LSD on normals. *Archives of General Psychiatry, 17* (5), 521-532.

McHenry, H.M. (1974, March). The emergence of man. By John E. Pfeiffer. *American Journal of Physical Anthropology, 40*(2), 295–296.

McMurray G.A. (1950). Experimental study of a case of insensitivity to pain. *Archives of Neurology and Psychiatry, 64*: 650-67

Miller, N.E. (1961). Learning and performance motivated by direct stimulation of the brain. In *Electrical Stimulation of the Brain*, D. E. Sheer (ed.). Austin, Texas: University of Texas Press.

Mindfulness: getting started. (n.d.). Retrieved from https://www.mindful.org/meditation/mindfulness-getting-started/

Nilus, A. (1975). *The Sayings of the Desert Fathers.* Sr. Benedicta Ward, Kalamazoo, Michigan: Cistercian Publications

Olds J. (1956, October). Pleasure centers in the brain. *Scientific American,195*, 105–116.

Olds, J., & Milner P. (1954). Positive reinforcement produced by electrical stimulation of septal area and other regions of rat brain. *Journal of Comparative and Physiological Psychology, 47*, 419–427.

Olds, J. & Olds, M. E. (1961). *Interference and learning in paleocortical systems.* In *Brain mechanisms and learning* (J. Delafresnaye, A. Fessard, and J. Konorski, editors). London, Great Britain: Blackwell Scientific Publications

Organ, T.W. (1970). *The Hindu quest for the perfection of man.* Columbus, OH: Ohio University Press.

Orpheus. (2015). *The Hymns of Orpheus - Scholar's Choice Edition.* Scholar's Choice.

Pahnke, W.N. (1966). Drugs and mysticism. *International Journal of Parapsychology, 8,* 295-320

Palmer, G.E.H., & Kadloubovsky, E. (1977). *Writings from the Philokalia on prayer of the heart.* London, Great Britain: Faber and Faber. Retrieved from http://trove.nla.gov.au/work/7678622

Papez, J.W. (1937). A proposed mechanism of emotion. *Archives of Neurology and Psychiatry, 38,* 725-743.

Patrushev, P. (2005). *Prigovoren k rasstrelu.* [Sentenced to Death]. St. Petersburg, Russia: Neva.

Patrushev, P. (2014). *Project Nirvana: How the War on Drugs Was Won* (2nd ed.). Sacramento, CA: Leaf Garden Press.

Patrushev, P. (2017). *Buddha's Balalaika.* Sacramento, CA: Leaf Garden Press.

Patrushev, P. *Burping and enlightenment: The hidden link* [web blog post]. (n.d.). Retrieved from http://goo.gl/NPtrJJ

Patrushev, P. (n.d.). *Nobel Prize won for psychedelic meditation breakthrough.* Retrieved from https://www.slideshare.net/alice_messerer/nobel-prize-won-for-psychedelic-meditation-breakthrough-slides-by-pyotr-patrushev

Patrushev, P. *Students combine meditation and mushrooms to go into the "genius" range* [Web blog post]. (n.d.). Retrieved from http://wardrugsnirvana.blogspot.com/2014/11/students-combine-meditation-and.html

Penfield, W. (2015). *Mystery of the mind: A critical study of consciousness and the human brain.* Princeton, NJ: Princeton University Press.

Penfield, W. (1958). *The excitable cortex in conscious man.* Liverpool, United Kingdom: Liverpool University Press.

Perry, J.W. (1989). *The far side of madness* (repr. ed.). Washington, DC: Spring Publications Incorporated.

Perry, J.W. (1999). *Trials of the visionary mind: spiritual emergency and the renewal process*. Albany, NY: State University of New York Press.

Pine, R. (trans.). (2013). *The Lankavatara Sutra: Translation and Commentary*. Berkeley, CA: Counterpoint.

Pirajno, A.D. di. (1955). *A cure for serpents* (1st Eng. ed.). New York, NY: Andre Deutsch.

Prabhupâda, A.C.B.S. (1990). *The journey of self-discovery* (later ed.). Los Angeles, CA: The Bhaktivedanta Book Trust.

Prabhupada, A.C.B.S. (2002). *The nectar of devotion*. Los Angeles, CA: The Bhaktivedanta Book Trust.

Prabhupada, A.C.B.S (2008). *Bhagavad Gita as it is*. (H. Das, ed.) (1st ed.). Krishna Books Incorporated.

Prabhupada, A.C.B.S. (1993). *Krsna: Pt. 1: the supreme personality of Godhead* (New ed.). Los Angeles, CA: Bhaktivedanta Book Trust.

Premack, A.J. Premack, D. (1972). Teaching language to an ape. *Scientific American, 227* (4), 92-99

Rachman, S. (1974). *The meanings of fear*. Harmondsworth, United Kingdom: Penguin Books.

Rheinhold H. (1950). UWSP Photo by Doug Moore. [© Axel Schmetzke, 2006]. Reprinted with kind permission of the copyright holder. Retrieved from https://library.uwsp.edu/aschmetz/Rheinhold%27s_Monkey/Rheinhold%27s_Monkey_Page.htm

Richter, C.P. (1957). On the Phenomenon of Sudden Death in Animals and Man. *Psychosomatic Medicine, 19*, 191–198.

Romer, A.S. (1960). *Man and the vertebrates*. Harmondsworth, Middlesex, Great Britain: Penguin Books

Ross, A.V. (1968). *Bombay after dark*. New York, NY: Macfadden-Bartell.

Russel, W.R. (1959). *Brain memory learning*. Oxford, Great Britain: Clarendon Press.

Sargant, W.W. (1957). Battle for the mind : a physiology of conversion and brain-washing (1st ed.). Garden City, NY : Doubleday.

Sargant, W., & Walters, W. (1973). *The mind possessed : a physiology of possession, mysticism and faith healing*. London, Great Britain: Heinemann.

Sartre, J., & Alexander, L. (2007). *Nausea*. New York, NY: New Direction.

Seligman, M.E.P. & Hager, J.L. (1972). *Biological boundaries of learning*. New York, NY: Appleton-Century-Crofts.

Selye, H. (1956). What is stress. *Metabolism*, 5: 595.

Schachter, S. & Singer J. (1962, September). Cognitive, social and physiological determinants of emotional state. *Psychological Review*, 69: 379-399.

Shovron, H.J. & Sargant, W. (1947). Excitatory Abreaction. *Journal of Mental Sciences*, 93: 709-732.

Simeons, A.T.W. (1961). *Man's presumptuous brain: An evolutionary interpretation of psychosomatic disease*. Boston, MA: Dutton.

Spiegel, H. (1977, October). The Hypnotic induction profile (hip): A review of its development. *Annals of the New York Academy of Sciences, 296*(1), 129–142.

Spuhler, J.N. (1973). Somatic paths to culture. In *Man in Evolutionary Perspective*. C. L. Brace and J. Metress (Eds.). New York, NY: John Wiley

Stanley-Jones, D. (1970). *The biological origins of love and hate. Feelings and Emotions*. (M.B. Arnold ed.) New York, NY: Academic. Staub, Ervin

Stein, L. (1971). Neurochemistry of reward and punishment some implications for the etiology of schizophrenia. *Journal of Psychiatric Research, 8*(3-4), 0-361

Steuart, R.H.J. (1999). *Mystical doctrine of St. John of the Cross*. London, Great Britain: Sheed & Ward.

Strassman, R.J. (1991). Human hallucinogenic drug research in the United States: a present-day case history and review of the process. *Journals of Psychoactive Drug*, 23, 29–38

Tart, C.T. (1972). States of consciousness and state-specific Sciences. *Science, 176*, 1203-10.

Tart, C.T. (1990). *Altered states of consciousness* (3rd rev. ed.). San Francisco, CA: Harper.

Temkin, O. (1994). *The Falling Sickness: A History of epilepsy from the Greeks to the beginnings of modern neurology* (Rev. ed.). Baltimore MD: Johns Hopkins University Press.

Thérèse, S., de Lisieux, & Edmonson, R. J. (2006). *The story of a soul : St. Thérèse of Lisieux, a new translation* (Complete & unabridged [ed.]). Brewster, MA : Paraclete Press.

Valentine, C. (1930). The innate causes of fear. *Journal of Genetic Psychology, 37*, 394-419.

Valentstein, E.S., & Beer, B. (1964). *Continuous opportunity for reinforcing brain stimulation. Journal of the Experimental Analysis of Behavior, 7*, 183–184.

Valenstein E.S. (1973). *Brain control*. New York, NY: Wiley.

Vasu, S.C. *(1974). The Gheranda samhita. New York*: AMS *Press*.

Veith, I. (1965). *Hysteria the history of a disease*. Chicago, ILL: Chicago University of Chicago Press.

Viegas, J. *Half of All Marine Life Lost in Just 40 Years*. [web blog post]. (2015). Retrieved from http://goo.gl/TbV9ZR

Walter, W.G. (1963). *The living brain*. New York, NY: W.W. Norton.

Washburg, C. (1961). *Primitive drinking: A study of the uses and functions of alcohol in preliterate societies*. New York, NY: College and University Press.

Watson, J. & Rayner, R. (1917). Emotional reactions and psychological experimentation. *American Journal of Psychology, 28*, 163-174.

Weith, I. (1965). *Hysteria: The History of a Disease*. Chicago, IL: University of Chicago Press.

Whytt, R. (2013). *Observations on the nature, causes, and cure of those disorders which have been commonly called nervous, hypochondriac, or hysteric: to which are ... of the nerves - primary source edition*. Charleston, SC: Nabu Press.

Williams, P. (2005). *Notes upon a case of obsessional neurosis*. In R. J. Perelberg (Ed.), Freud (177–188). Hoboken, NJ: Whurr Publishers Ltd. Retrieved from https://doi.org/10.1002/9780470713525.ch10

Yogi, M. M. (2001). *Science of Being and Art of Living: Transcendental Meditation* (rev. & upd. Ed.). New York, N.Y.: Plume.

Young, J.Z. (1965). The organization of a memory system. *Proceedings of the Royal Society, 163*B, 285-320.

Zaehner, R.C. (1978). *Mysticism - sacred and profane - an inquiry into some varieties of praeternatural experience*. Oxford, Great Britain: Oxford University Press.

Zaehner, R.C. (1989). *Zen, drugs, and mysticism by* Paperback. UPA.

Zondervan (2010). *Holy Bible, King James Version*. Grand Rapids, MI: Zondervan.

www.ingramcontent.com/pod-product-compliance
Lightning Source LLC
Chambersburg PA
CBHW071500040426
42444CB00008B/1433